《实用汉语课本》第一册

# 汉字练习本

## CHINESE CHARACTER
## EXERCISE BOOK

FOR
PRACTICAL CHINESE READER
BOOK I

北 京 语 言 学 院

刘 珣 邓恩明 刘社会 编著
李培元 审订

THE COMMERCIAL PRESS

1999 Beijing

Published by the Commercial Press,
36 Wanfujing Street, Beijing, China
Typeset by the Beijing Languages
Institute Printing House,
Beijing, China
Distributed by China International Book Trading Corporation
(GUOJI SHUDIAN)
P. O. Box 399, Beijing, China

*Printed in the People's Republic of China*

# 说　明

　　《汉字练习本》是《实用汉语课本》第一、二册的辅助材料，是为了帮助外国读者解决汉字难认、难写、难记的困难而编写的。我们根据对外国学生教学汉字的经验，编写了一些关于汉字结构规律的基本知识，并采用外国人学习汉字行之有效的练习方式，以培养和提高外国读者认、写汉字的能力。

　　限于水平，不足之处，在所难免，望批评指正。

　　本书的英文翻译是何培慧。插图是张志忠。

编　者

1981 年 12 月

# Explanatory Notes

This *Chinese Character Exercise Book*, which consists of two volumes, is a supplement to *Practical Chinese Reader* (Book I & II). It has been compiled for the express purpose of helping foreigners to learn Chinese characters which are difficult to identify, write and memorize. We have summed up elementary knowledge concerning the structure of Chinese characters based on our past experience in teaching foreigners, and have adopted methods in the exercises which have proved to be effective in teaching our students to acquire proficiency in identifying and writing characters.

Users are cordially invited to make corrections and suggestions which will help us to improve our revision of this exercise book.

The English translation was by He Peihui and illustrations by Zhang Zhizhong.

The compilers

December, 1981

# 目　录
## CONTENTS

# 第 一 课　Lesson 1

一、汉字分析

**Analysis of Characters**

1) 笔画

**Character strokes**

汉字是由不同笔画构成的。写字的时候，由落笔到停笔，叫作"一笔"或"一画"。例如：

Chinese characters are composed of different types of strokes. A stroke is the single unbroken line drawn by the writer from the time he sets his pen to paper and moves it till the time he lifts it off paper. E.g.

丿（ノ）——撇，由右上向左下。如果由左下向右上，就变成另一种笔画。〔乀（㇏）〕。

A *pie* or left-falling stroke "丿（ノ）", written from top-right to bottom-left. It will become the stroke "乀（㇏）" if written the other way round.

丨（↓）——竖，由上向下，不能由下向上。

A *shu* or vertical stroke "丨（↓）", written from top to bottom, never the other way round.

一（ㄱ）——横钩，先由左向右，到笔画转弯时要很快提笔。

A *henggou* or horizontal hook stroke "⌐ (ᄀ)", written first from left to right, then lifting the pen as quickly as possible to make the hook.

亅(亅)——竖钩，先由上向下，到笔画转弯时要很快提笔。

A *shugou* or vertical hook stroke "亅 (亅)", written first downward, then lifting the pen as quickly as possible to make the hook.

丶(丶)——左点，由右向左点一下。

A *zuodian* or left-falling dot stroke "丶(丶)", written from right to bottom-left.

丶(丶)——右点，由左向右点一下。

A *youdian* or right-falling dot stroke "丶 (丶)", written from left to bottom-right.

く(く)——撇点，由右上向左下再向右，相当于"丿"和"丶"两种笔画的合成，不能写成两笔。

A *piedian* or left-falling stroke plus right-falling dot stroke "く(く)", written first from top-right to bottom-left, then to right. This stroke is about the same as the combination of the two strokes "丿" and "、", but it must be written as one single unbroken stroke instead of two separate strokes.

一 (→) ——横，由左向右，不能由右向左。

A *heng* or horizontal stroke "— (→)", written from left to right, never the other way round.

亅 (亅) ——弯钩，由上向下稍弯，到笔画转弯时，要很快提笔。

A *wangou* or crooked hook stroke "亅, (亅)", written from top to bottom with a slight hook, then lifting the pen as quickly as possible to make the hook.

2) 汉字偏旁

Character component

在汉字形体中常常出现的某些组成部分，如"好"字中的"女"和"子"就是偏旁。

The component parts making up a Chinese character are known as character components, as "女" and "子" in the character "好".

你 { 亻 (单立人 dānlìrén the component "亻")
      尔

几　亻（人）　古字象一人侧立。

The component "亻" is a variant of the character "人" which originated from the above ideogram symbolizing a person standing sideways.

单立人旁的字都和人有关。

A character containing the "亻" component usually has a human connotation.

二、汉字练习

Character Exercises:

1. 汉字认读：

Character recognition

你　好

2. 按正确写法描写下列笔画：

Trace the following strokes in the correct way:

| | | | | | | |
|---|---|---|---|---|---|---|
| ノ | ノ | ノ | ノ | ノ | ノ | ノ |
| 丶 | 丶 | 丶 | 丶 | 丶 | 丶 | 丶 |
| 一 | 一 | 一 | 一 | 一 | 一 | 一 |
| 丨 | 丨 | 丨 | 丨 | 丨 | 丨 | 丨 |
| 丿 | 丿 | 丿 | 丿 | 丿 | 丿 | 丿 |

| | | | | | | |
|---|---|---|---|---|---|---|
| ➚ | ➚ | ➚ | ➚ | ➚ | ➚ | ➚ |
| ↓ | ↓ | ↓ | ↓ | ↓ | ↓ | ↓ |
| ) | ) | ) | ) | ) | ) | ) |
| ︿ | ︿ | ︿ | ︿ | ︿ | ︿ | ︿ |

按正确写法临写下列笔画:

Copy the following strokes in the correct way:

| | | | | | |
|---|---|---|---|---|---|
| ✓ | | | | | |
| 、 | | | | | |
| 一 | | | | | |
| 丨 | | | | | |
| 丿 | | | | | |
| ➚ | | | | | |
| ↓ | | | | | |
| ) | | | | | |

| ㇂ | | | | | | |
|---|---|---|---|---|---|---|

3. 数一数下列汉字的笔画，把结果写在（　）中：

Count the strokes each of the following characters contains and put the number in the brackets:

你（　）　好（　）

按正确笔顺描写下列汉字：

Trace the following characters in the correct stroke-order:

| 你 | ノ | 亻 | 仵 | 仸 | 佑 | 你 |
|---|---|---|---|---|---|---|
| 你 | 你 | 你 | 你 | 你 | 你 | nǐ |
| 好 | ㇛ | 乆 | 女 | 女'' | 奵 | 好 |
| 好 | 好 | 好 | 好 | 好 | 好 | hǎo |

4. 按正确笔顺临写下列汉字：

Copy the following characters in the correct stroke-order:

| 你 | | | | | | |
|---|---|---|---|---|---|---|
| 好 | | | | | | |

5. 把下列词语中的拼音写成汉字：

Put the phonetic transcriptinos in the following
sentences into Chinese characters:

Nǐ＿＿好。

你 hǎo＿＿。

Nǐ hǎo＿＿＿＿。

# 第 二 课　Lesson 2

一、汉字分析

Analysis of Characters

1. 笔画

Character strokes

㇏（丿）——提，由左下向右上。如果由右上向左下，就变成〔丿（㇒）〕。

A *ti* or rising stroke "㇏ （丿）", written from bottom-left to top-right. It will become the left-falling stroke "丿 （㇒）" if written the other way round.

我

丶（㇏）——捺，由左上向右下，不能由左下向左上。

A *na* or right-falling stroke " 丶 （㇏）", written from top-left to bottom-right, never the other way round.

很

乚（乚）——斜钩，由左上斜向右下，再向上很快提笔。

A *xiegou* or slanting hook stroke "乀 (乚)", written first from top-left to bottom-right, then lifting the pen upward as quickly as possible to make a hook at the end.

フ (フ)──横折，由左向右再向左下，不要写成直角，也与"一"不同。

A *hengzhe* or horizontal turning stroke "フ (フ)", written from left to right and then to bottom-left. Notice that this stroke is written with an acute instead of a right angle, and it is also somewhat different from the stroke "一".

乛 (乛)──横折钩，可看作是"一"和"亅"的结合，但必须一笔写成，如"也"。

A *hengzhegou* "乛 (乛)". This stroke may be said to be a combination of the strokes "一" and "亅", but it must be written as a single unbroken stroke instead of separate strokes, as in "也".

乚 (乚)──竖弯钩，可看作是"丨"和"乚"的结合，但必须一笔写成，如"也"。

A *shuwangou* "乚 (乚)". This stroke is something like a combination of the strokes "丨" and "乚", but it must also be written as a single unbroken stroke, as in "也".

ㄣ (ㄣ)──竖折折钩。，可看作是"乚"和"乀"的结合，但必须一笔写成，如"吗"。

A *shuzhezhegou* "⅃ (⅃)". This stroke is a combination of the strokes "∟" and "亅", but it must be written also as a single unbroken stroke, as in "吗".

丨 (亅)——竖提。

A *shuti* or vertical rising stroke "丨 (亅)".

## 2. 汉字偏旁
Character component

吗 { 口 (口字旁 kǒuzìpáng the component "口") 马

口 古字象口。

The component "口" came from the ideogram on the left symbolizing mouth.

口字旁的字大都是与口有关，如"吗"、"呢"是语气词，用口旁。

Therefore, the meaning of any character containing "口" usually has something to do with the mouth, e.g. "吗" and "呢", which are both modal particles.

二、汉字练习

10

**Character Exercises:**

1. 汉字认读：
   Character recognition:

   你好吗？
   我很好，你呢？
   也很好。

2. 按正确笔顺写出下列汉字的笔画：
   Write out the strokes each of the following characters
   contains in the correct stroke-order:

   例字：
   Example:

| 吗 | 丶 | 口 | 口 | 叮 | 吗 | 吗 | |
|---|---|---|---|---|---|---|---|

| 你 | | | | | | | |
|---|---|---|---|---|---|---|---|
| 好 | | | | | | | |

3. 按正确写法描写下列笔画：
   Trace the following strokes in the correct way:

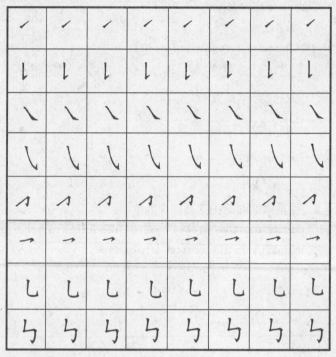

按正确写法临写下列笔画：

Copy the following strokes in the correct way:

| | | | | | | |
|---|---|---|---|---|---|---|
| ㇏ | | | | | | |
| ㄥ | | | | | | |
| ㇀ | | | | | | |
| ㄅ | | | | | | |

**4.** 数一数下列汉字的笔画，把结果写在（　　）中：

Count the strokes each of the following characters
contains and put the number in the brackets:

我（　　）很（　　）吗（　　）呢（　　）

按正确笔顺描写下列汉字：

Trace the following characters in the correct stroke-
order:

| 我 | ㇒ | 二 | 手 | 手 | 我 | 我 | 我 |
|---|---|---|---|---|---|---|---|
| 我 | 我 | 我 | 我 | 我 | 我 | wǒ | |
| 很 | ㇒ | ㇒ | 彳 | 彳 | 彳 | 彳 | 很 |
| 很 | 很 | 很 | 很 | 很 | 很 | hěn | |
| 也 | ㇇ | 力 | 也 | 也 | 也 | yě | |

| 吗 | ⼁ | ⼝ | ⼝ | 叼 | 吗 | 吗 | 吗 |
|---|---|---|---|---|---|---|---|
| 吗 | 吗 | 吗 | 吗 | 吗 | 吗 | ma | |
| 呢 | 口ㄱ | 口ㄱ | 呀 | 呢 | 呢 | ne | |

5. 给下列汉字注音，把相同的偏旁写在（  ）中：

Write out each of the following characters in phonetic transcription and put the common component they contain in the bracket:

吗＿＿＿＿＿＿   呢＿＿＿＿＿＿（     ）

6. 把下列对话中的拼音写成汉字：

Put the phonetic transcriptions in the following dialogue into Chinese characters:

A. 你好ma ＿＿＿＿＿？

B. Hěn ＿＿＿＿＿好，你ne＿＿＿＿＿？

A. Wǒ ＿＿＿＿＿yě＿＿＿＿＿很好。

14

# 第 三 课  Lesson 3

一、汉字分析

Analysis of Characters

1. 笔画

Character strokes

阝（ꝫ）——横撇弯钩，可看作是"⁊"和"ꝫ"的结合，但必须一笔写成，如"都"。

A *hengpiewangou* "ꝫ（ꝫ）". This stroke is something like a combination of the strokes "⁊" and "ꝫ" written as one unbroken stroke, as in "都"：

乛（ꝗ）——横折钩，可看作是"一"和"丨"的结合，但必须一笔写成，如"门"。

A *hengzhegou* "乛（ꝗ）". This stroke is something like a combination of the strokes "一" and "丨" written as one continuous stroke, as in "们"：

ㄴ（ㄴ）——竖折，如"忙"。

A *shuzhe* or vertical turning stroke "ㄴ（ㄴ）", as in "忙".

15

2. 汉字偏旁

Character component

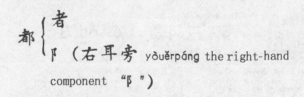

都 { 者
    阝 (右耳旁 yòuěrpáng the right-hand
    component "阝")

二、汉字练习

Character Exercises

1. 汉字认读：

Character recognition：

哥哥忙，弟弟忙，他们都很忙。
你很忙，他也很忙，我不忙。

认读下列各偏旁的汉字：

Read out the following groups of characters containing
one component in common:

亻：你　他　们
口：吗　呢

2. 按正确笔顺写出下列汉字的笔画：

Write out the strokes each of the following characters
contains in the correct stroke-order;

| 我 | | | | | | | |
| 很 | | | | | | | |
| 吗 | | | | | | | |
| 呢 | | | | | | | |

**3. 按正确写法描写下列笔画：**

Trace the following strokes in the correct way:

| ㇠ | ㇠ | ㇠ | ㇠ | ㇠ | ㇠ | ㇠ | ㇠ |
| 𠃌 | 𠃌 | 𠃌 | 𠃌 | 𠃌 | 𠃌 | 𠃌 | 𠃌 |
| ㄴ | ㄴ | ㄴ | ㄴ | ㄴ | ㄴ | ㄴ | ㄴ |
| ㇉ | ㇉ | ㇉ | ㇉ | ㇉ | ㇉ | ㇉ | ㇉ |
| ㇄ | ㇄ | ㇄ | ㇄ | ㇄ | ㇄ | ㇄ | ㇄ |
| ㇀ | ㇀ | ㇀ | ㇀ | ㇀ | ㇀ | ㇀ | ㇀ |
| ㇀ | ㇀ | ㇀ | ㇀ | ㇀ | ㇀ | ㇀ | ㇀ |

按正确写法临写下列笔画：
Copy the following strokes in the correct way:

| | | | | | | |
|---|---|---|---|---|---|---|
| ㇌ | | | | | | |
| ㇆ | | | | | | |
| ㇗ | | | | | | |
| ㇥ | | | | | | |
| ㇠ | | | | | | |
| ㇡ | | | | | | |
| ㇁ | | | | | | |
| ㇀ | | | | | | |

4. 数一数下列汉字的笔画，把结果写在（  ）中：
   Count the strokes each of the following characters
   contains and put the number in the brackets:

哥（  ）  弟（  ）  都（  ）

按正确笔顺描写下列汉字：

18

Trace the following characters in the correct stroke-order:

| | | | | | |
|---|---|---|---|---|---|
| 哥 | 一 | 口 | 可 | 可 | 哥 | gē |
| 弟 | 丶 | 丷 | 艹 | 当 | 弟 | 弟 |
| 弟 | 弟 | 弟 | 弟 | 弟 | 弟 | dì |
| 他 | 亻 | 他 | 他 | 他 | 他 | tā |
| 们 | 亻 | 忄 | 们 | 们 | 们 | mén |
| 不 | 一 | 丆 | 不 | 不 | 不 | bù |
| 忙 | 丶 | 丨 | 忄 | 忙 | 忙 | 忙 |
| 忙 | 忙 | 忙 | 忙 | 忙 | 忙 | máng |
| 都 | 一 | 十 | 土 | 耂 | 者 | 者 |
| 者 | 都 | 都 | 都 | 都 | 都 | dōu |

5. 把下列句子中的拼音写成汉字：
   Put the phonetic transcriptions in the following sentences into Chinese characters:

19

gēge _____ 很忙，

dìdi _____ 也很忙，

他们 dōu _____ 很 máng _____。

我 bù _____ 忙。

# 第 四 课  Lesson 4

一、汉字分析

Analysis of Characters

1. 笔画

Character strokes

ㄋ（ㄋ）——横折折撇，可看作是"フ"和"フ"的结合，但必须
一笔写成，如"这"。

A *hengzhezhepie* "ㄋ（ㄋ）". This stroke is
something like a combination of the strokes
"フ" and "フ" written as a single unbroken
stroke, as in "这".

フ（フ）——横撇，可看作是"－"和"丿"的结合，但必须一笔
写成，如"友"。

A *hengpie* "フ（フ）". This stroke is something
like a conbination of the strokes "－" and
"丿" written as a single unbroken stroke, as
in "友".

乀（乀）——平捺，如"这"。

A *pingna* or level right-falling stroke "乀
（乀）", as in "这".

## 2．汉字偏旁
### Character component

$$妈 \begin{cases} 女 \text{（女字旁 nǚzìpáng the component "女"）} \\ 马 \end{cases}$$

女字旁的字大都和女性有关，如"妈妈"。

A character containing "女" usually has a connotation pertaining to a female person, e.g."妈妈".

## 二、汉字练习
### Character Exercises

### 1．认读下列女字旁的汉字：
Read out the following characters containing the component "女":

女：妈妈　好

### 2．认读下列词和句子：
Read out the following words and sentences:

爸爸　妈妈　哥哥　弟弟　朋友
这是我朋友。我们都很好。

### 3．按正确写法描写下列笔画：
Trace the following strokes in the correct way:

| 乛 | 乛 | 乛 | 乛 | 乛 | 乛 | 乛 | 乛 |
|---|---|---|---|---|---|---|---|
| ㄱ | ㄱ | ㄱ | ㄱ | ㄱ | ㄱ | ㄱ | ㄱ |

| | | | | | | | |
|---|---|---|---|---|---|---|---|
| ⌣ | ⌣ | ⌣ | ⌣ | ⌣ | ⌣ | ⌣ | ⌣ |
| 乛 | 乛 | 乛 | 乛 | 乛 | 乛 | 乛 | 乛 |
| フ | フ | フ | フ | フ | フ | フ | フ |
| ⺄ | ⺄ | ⺄ | ⺄ | ⺄ | ⺄ | ⺄ | ⺄ |
| ノ | ノ | ノ | ノ | ノ | ノ | ノ | ノ |
| ㇆ | ㇆ | ㇆ | ㇆ | ㇆ | ㇆ | ㇆ | ㇆ |
| ㇏ | ㇏ | ㇏ | ㇏ | ㇏ | ㇏ | ㇏ | ㇏ |

按正确写法临写下列笔画：

Copy the following strokes in the correct way:

| | | | | | | | |
|---|---|---|---|---|---|---|---|
| 乛 | | | | | | | |
| 乛 | | | | | | | |
| フ | | | | | | | |
| ⌣ | | | | | | | |
| ㇏ | | | | | | | |

4. 按正确笔顺描写下列汉字：

Trace the following characters in the correct stroke-order:

| | | | | | | |
|---|---|---|---|---|---|---|
| 这 | 丶 | 二 | 亍 | 文 | 讠文 | 讠 | 这 |
| 这 | 这 | 这 | 这 | 这 | 这 | zhè | |
| 是 | 丨 | 口 | 日 | 旦 | 早 | 昗 | |
| 昗 | 是 | 是 | 是 | 是 | 是 | shì | |
| 爸 | 丿 | 八 | 分 | 父 | 爷 | 爷 | 爸 |
| 爸 | 爸 | 爸 | 爸 | 爸 | 爸 | bà | |
| 妈 | 女 | 妈 | 妈 | 妈 | 妈 | mā | |
| 朋 | 丿 | 刀 | 月 | 月 | 朋 | péng | |
| 友 | 一 | 广 | 方 | 友 | 友 | yǒu | |

5. 给下列形近字注音，并组成词语写在（　　　）里：

Write in phonetic transcription the characters similar in shape and structure in each pair, then make up words or phrases with each and put what you have made in the brackets:

吗＿＿＿＿（　　　　）妈＿＿＿＿（　　　　）

6. 给下列各组汉字注音，把相同的偏旁写在（　　）中：
Write each of the following characters in phonetic transcription and put in the brackets the component that the characters in each group have in common:

妈＿＿＿好＿＿＿（　　　　）

吗＿＿＿呢＿＿＿（　　　　）

你＿＿＿他＿＿＿们（　　　　）

7. 把下列拼音写成汉字：
Put the phonetic transcriptions in the following sentences into Chinese characters:

你 hǎo＿＿＿＿吗？

他 hěnmáng＿＿＿＿＿＿。

Zhè＿＿＿ shì＿＿＿我 péng＿＿＿友。

# 第 五 课　Lesson 5

一、汉字分析
Analysis of Characters

  車　车

横看象车的形状。

The component "车" is the simplified form of the character "車", originated from the above ideogram symbolizing a cart.

二、汉字练习
Character Exercises

1. 汉字认读：
Character recognition:

1) 辨认下列形近字：
Identify the characters similar in shape and structure in each pair:

大———夫　　妈———吗

2) 认读句子：

26

Read out the following sentences:

她是大夫。

这是她的车。

那是她的书。

妈妈是她的朋友。

2. 按正确笔顺描写下列汉字：
Trace the following characters in the correct stroke-order:

| | | | | | | |
|---|---|---|---|---|---|---|
| 她 | 女 | 她 | 她 | 她 | 她 | tā |
| 那 | 刁 | 刁 | 刍 | 月 | 邧 | 那 |
| 那 | 那 | 那 | 那 | 那 | 那 | nà |
| 车 | 一 | 七 | 车 | 车 | 车 | chē |
| 大 | 一 | 十 | 大 | 大 | 大 | dài |
| 夫 | 一 | 二 | 丰 | 夫 | 夫 | fū |
| 的 | ノ | 亻 | 白 | 白 | 白 | 的 |

| | | | | | | |
|---|---|---|---|---|---|---|
| 的 | 的 | 的 | 的 | 的 | 的 | de |
| 书 | ㄱ | ㄢ | 书 | 书 | 书 | shū |

**3. 按笔顺写出下列汉字的笔画:**

write out the strokes making up the following characters in the correct stroke-order:

| | | | | | | |
|---|---|---|---|---|---|---|
| 那 | | | | | | |
| 是 | | | | | | |
| 我 | | | | | | |
| 的 | | | | | | |
| 书 | | | | | | |
| 吗 | | | | | | |

**4. 临写下列汉字，注意笔画在田字格中的位置:**

Copy each of the following characters, paying attention to the position of each stroke in the crossed
square:

| 她 | | | | | | | |
|---|---|---|---|---|---|---|---|
| 那 | | | | | | | |
| 大 | | | | | | | |
| 夫 | | | | | | | |
| 的 | | | | | | | |
| 车 | | | | | | | |
| 书 | | | | | | | |

5. 把下列拼音写成汉字：
   Put the following phonetic transcriptions into Chinese characters:

tāmen ＿＿＿＿＿  ⎫
nǐmen ＿＿＿＿＿  ⎬ 的书
wǒmen ＿＿＿＿＿  ⎭

dàifu ＿＿＿＿＿  ⎫
péngyou ＿＿＿＿  ⎬ 的车
            ⎭

6. 给下列各组汉字注音，把相同的偏旁写在（　　）中：
   Write each of the following characters in phonetic transcription and put in the brackets the component that the characters in each group have in common:

那＿＿＿＿＿都＿＿＿＿＿（　　）
她＿＿＿＿＿妈＿＿＿好＿＿＿（　　）

# 第 六 课  Lesson 6

一、汉字分析

Analysis of Characters

汉字偏旁

Character components

$$语 \begin{cases} 讠 & （言字旁 \; yánzìpáng \; the \; component "讠"） \\ 吾 \end{cases}$$

言字旁的字大都与言语有关。汉语的"语"字用言旁。

The meaning of any character containing the component "讠" mostly has something to do with speech or language, as in "语".

$$国 \begin{cases} 囗 & （国字框 \; guózìkuàng \; the \; component "囗"） \\ 玉 \end{cases}$$

"囗"表示范围和四边的界限。

The component "囗" indicates an enclosed space and its boundary lines.

二、汉字练习

Character Exercises

1. 汉字认读：

Character recognition:

1) 认读下列各偏旁的汉字：

Read out the characters containing each of the
following components given at the head of each
group:

讠：语　谁

口：哪　吗　呢

2) 认读下列词语：

Read out the following words and phrases:

们：你们　我们　他们　她们

老师们　大夫们　朋友们

2. 按正确写法描写下列笔画：

Trace the following strokes in the correct way:

| | | | | | | | |
|---|---|---|---|---|---|---|---|
| ㇡ | ㇡ | ㇡ | ㇡ | ㇡ | ㇡ | ㇡ | ㇡ |
| ㇆ | ㇆ | ㇆ | ㇆ | ㇆ | ㇆ | ㇆ | ㇆ |
| ㇌ | ㇌ | ㇌ | ㇌ | ㇌ | ㇌ | ㇌ | ㇌ |
| ㇀ | ㇀ | ㇀ | ㇀ | ㇀ | ㇀ | ㇀ | ㇀ |

按正确的笔顺描写下列汉字：
Trace the following characters in the correct stroke-order:

| | | | | | | |
|---|---|---|---|---|---|---|
| 谁 | 丶 | 讠 | 计 | 计 | 许 | 诈 |
| 谁 | 谁 | 谁 | 谁 | 谁 | 谁 | sheí |
| 老 | 一 | 十 | 土 | 耂 | 耂 | 老 |
| 老 | 老 | 老 | 老 | 老 | 老 | lǎo |
| 师 | 丨 | 丿 | 厂 | 归 | 师 | 师 |
| 师 | 师 | 师 | 师 | 师 | 师 | shī |
| 哪 | 口 | 哪 | 哪 | 哪 | 哪 | nǎ |
| 国 | 丨 | 冂 | 冂 | 冃 | 用 | 国 |
| 国 | 国 | 国 | 国 | 国 | 国 | guó |

33

| 人 | ノ | 人 | 人 | 人 | 人 | rén |
|---|---|---|---|---|---|---|
| 汉 | 丶 | 丶丶 | 氵 | 汈 | 汉 | hàn |
| 语 | 讠 | 订 | 订 | 诏 | 语 | 语 |
| 语 | 语 | 语 | 语 | 语 | 语 | yǔ |

3. 临写下列汉字，注意笔画在田字格中的位置：
Copy each of the following characters, paying
attention to the position of each stroke in the crossed
square:

| 汉 | | | | | | |
|---|---|---|---|---|---|---|
| 语 | | | | | | |
| 老 | | | | | | |
| 师 | | | | | | |
| 哪 | | | | | | |
| 国 | | | | | | |

| 人 | | | | | | | | |
|---|---|---|---|---|---|---|---|---|

**4.** 给下列各组汉字注音，把相同的偏旁写在（　）中：
Transcribe the following characters and put in the brackets the component that the characters in each group have in common:

语＿＿＿＿　谁＿＿＿＿（　　　）

哪＿＿＿＿　那＿＿＿＿　都＿＿＿＿（　　　）

**5.** 读拼音写出汉字：
Read out the following phonetic transcriptions and put them into Chinese characters:

1) wǒ＿＿＿们　　　nǐ＿＿＿们

tā＿＿＿们　　　tā＿＿＿们

2) Hànyǔ＿＿＿＿Lǎoshī＿＿＿＿shì＿＿＿＿

Zhōngguó＿＿＿＿rén.＿＿＿＿。

# 第 七 课  Lesson 7

一、汉字分析

Analysis of Characters

1. 汉字偏旁

Character component

看 {
严

目 (目字底 mùzìdǐ the component "目")

目　　横看象眼睛。

The component "目" was derived from the ancient ideogram on the left symbolizing the eye.

目字底或目字旁的字大都与眼睛的名称和动作有关。"看"字上边是手，下边是目字底。手放在眼睛上表示看。

The meaning of any character containing the component "目" usually has something to do with the eyes or their functions. The character "看", for example, composed of "手" (a hand) shading "目" (an eye), signifies "look",

36

地 { 土（土字旁 tǔzìpáng the component "土"）
也

2. **笔画**　汉字基本笔画是点"、"，横"一"，竖"｜"，撇
"丿"，捺"乀"，提"㇀"六种。由两种或两种以上的
基本笔画联合起来，又形成有折笔的复杂笔画。这类笔
画我们大部分已学过，现归纳如下：

Character strokes: The six basic strokes making up
Chinese characters are "、" (the dot stroke), "—" (the
horizontal stroke), "｜" (the vertical stroke), "丿" (the
left-falling stroke), "乀" (the right-falling stroke) and
"㇀"(the rising stroke). All others are complicated strokes, or
those containing hooks or turnings, formed of two or more
basic strokes. Here is a list of both types of strokes most
of which have been already dealt with:

| 笔画<br>Strokes | 名　　称<br>Names | 例字<br>Examples |
|---|---|---|
| 、 | 点 diǎn | 不 |
| 一 | 横 héng | 大 |
| ｜ | 竖 shù | 中 |
| 丿 | 撇 piě | 么 |

| | | |
|---|---|---|
| 乀 | 捺 nà | 人 |
| ノ | 提 tí | 汉 |
| ㄱ | 横折 héngzhé | 呢 |
| ｊ | 竖钩 shùgōu | 你 |
| く | 撇点 piědiǎn | 妈 |
| ノ | 竖撇 shùpiě | 朋 |
| フ | 横撇 héngpiě | 友 |
| ⁊ | 横折弯撇 héngzhéwānpiě | 这 |
| ⌒ | 平捺 píngnà | 这 |
| ㇄ | 竖提 shùtí | 很 |
| ⟍ | 横折提 héngzhétí | 语 |
| ㄥ | 撇折 piězhé | 么 |
| 乀 | 斜钩 xiégōu | 我 |

38

| | | |
|---|---|---|
| ） | 弯钩 wāngōu | 好 |
| ┐ | 横折钩 héngzhégōu | 们 |
| フ | 横钩 hénggōu | 你 |
| ㇇ | 横折钩 héngzhégōu | 他 |
| ㇄ | 竖弯钩 shùwāngōu | 也 |
| 勹 | 竖折折钩 shùzhézhégōu | 吗 |
| ㇋ | 横折折钩 héngzhézhégōu | 那 |

二、汉字练习

Character Exercises

1. 汉字认读：

Character recognition:

1) 辨认下列各组形近字：

Identify the characters similar in shape and structure in each of the following pairs:

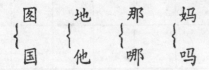

$$\left\{\begin{matrix}图\\国\end{matrix}\right. \quad \left\{\begin{matrix}地\\他\end{matrix}\right. \quad \left\{\begin{matrix}那\\哪\end{matrix}\right. \quad \left\{\begin{matrix}妈\\吗\end{matrix}\right.$$

2) 认读句子：

Read out the following sentences:

看什么？　　看地图。

什么地图？　　北京地图。

2. 数一数下列汉字的笔画，把结果写在（ ）中：

Count the strokes each of the following characters
contains and put the number of strokes in the
brackets:

我（　　） 弟（　　） 是（　　）

都（　　） 那（　　） 很（　　）

好（　　） 谁（　　） 图（　　）

老（　　） 哥（　　） 看（　　）

按笔顺写出下列汉字的笔画：

Write out the strokes each of the following characters
contains in the correct stroke-order:

| 他 | | | | | |
|---|---|---|---|---|---|
| 是 | | | | | |
| 汉 | | | | | |

| 语 | | | | | | |
|---|---|---|---|---|---|---|
| 老 | | | | | | |
| 师 | | | | | | |

**3. 按正确笔顺描写下列汉字：**

Trace the following characters in the correct stroke-order:

| 看 | 一 | 二 | 三 | 手 | 丢 | 看 | 看 |
|---|---|---|---|---|---|---|---|
| 看 | 看 | 看 | 看 | 看 | 看 | kàn | |
| 什 | 亻 | 仁 | 什 | 什 | 什 | shén | |
| 么 | 丿 | 厶 | 么 | 么 | 么 | me | |
| 地 | 一 | 士 | 圡 | 地 | 地 | dì | |
| 图 | 冂 | 门 | 冈 | 冈 | 图 | 图 | 图 |
| 图 | 图 | 图 | 图 | 图 | 图 | tú | |

**4. 给下列各组汉字注音，把相同的偏旁写在（　）中：**

41

Write each of the following characters in phonetic transcription and put in the brackets the common component contained in the characters in each gronp:

你＿＿＿ 他＿＿＿ 们＿＿＿ 什＿＿＿ （ ）

吗＿＿＿ 呢＿＿＿ 哪＿＿＿ （ ）

她＿＿＿ 妈＿＿＿ 好＿＿＿ （ ）

语＿＿＿ 谁＿＿＿ （ ）

都＿＿＿ 那＿＿＿ （ ）

国＿＿＿ 图＿＿＿ （ ）

5. 把下列拼音写成汉字：

Put the phonetic transcriptions in the following sentences into Chinese characters:

这是 shénme＿＿＿＿＿＿＿ 地 tú＿＿＿＿？

这是 Zhōngguó＿＿＿＿＿＿＿＿＿ dì＿＿＿ 图。

Nà＿＿＿ 是 lǎoshī＿＿＿＿＿＿ 的 Běijīng＿＿＿＿＿

地图。

你 kàn＿＿＿＿ 吗？

6. 写出带下列偏旁的汉字：

42

Write out the characters each containing one of the following components:

亻 ＿＿＿ ＿＿＿ ＿＿＿ ＿＿＿

讠 ＿＿＿ ＿＿＿

女 ＿＿＿ ＿＿＿

卩 ＿＿＿ ＿＿＿ ＿＿＿

囗 ＿＿＿ ＿＿＿

阝 ＿＿＿ ＿＿＿

7. 找出下列句子中的错别字并改正：
Pick out the wrongly written characters in the following sentences, then give the correct forms in the brackets:

他很忙。(　　　)

我木忙。(　　　)(　　　)

那是谁的书。(　　　)(　　　)(　　　)

# 第八课 Lesson 8

一、汉字分析

Analysis of Characters

1. 笔顺

Stroke-order:

一个字先写哪一笔，后写哪一笔，叫做笔顺。

The proper order in which the strokes
making up a character are written is known as
stroke-order.

汉字笔顺基本规则（一）：从上到下。先写上面的笔画和结构单位，再写下面的笔画和结构单位。例如：

Basic Stroke-order Rule (1): From top strokes to bottom
ones. Strokes forming the upper part of a component
or a character should precede those forming the lower
part. E.g.

京：　一　言　京

是：　日　是

茶：　艹　苶　茶

2. 汉字偏旁

Character component

进 { 井
     辶 （走之旁 zǒuzhīpáng the component "辶"）

走之旁的字大都与走的动作有关。

The meaning of any character containing "辶" usually
has something to do with walking or the motion of
walking.

二、汉字练习

**Character Exercises**

1. 汉字认读：

**Character recognition:**

1) 认读下列偏旁的汉字：

Read out the following characters that have one
component in common in each group:

辶： 进 迎 这

讠： 请 语 谢 谁

口： 喝 吗 呢 哪

2) 认读词语：

Read out the following words and phrases:

请： 请进 请喝茶 请看书

2. 按正确笔顺描写下列汉字：

Trace the following characters in the correct stroke-
order:

| 请 | 讠 | 计 | 订 | 讳 | 诗 | 请 | 请 |
| 请 | 请 | 请 | 请 | 请 | 请 | qǐng | |
| 喝 | 口 | 吧 | 呬 | 喝 | 喝 | 喝 | 喝 |
| 喝 | 喝 | 喝 | 喝 | 喝 | 喝 | hē | |
| 茶 | 一 | 一 | 艹 | 芡 | 苶 | 苯 | 茶 |
| 茶 | 茶 | 茶 | 茶 | 茶 | 茶 | chá | |
| 您 | 你 | 你 | 您 | 您 | 您 | nín | |
| 进 | 一 | 二 | 卡 | 井 | 进 | jìn | |
| 欢 | 又 | 又 | 欢 | 欢 | 欢 | huān | |
| 迎 | ノ | ㇉ | ㇉口 | 卬 | 迎 | yíng | |
| 谢 | 讠 | 订 | 讠寸 | 讷 | 讷 | 讷 | 讷 |

| | | | | | | |
|---|---|---|---|---|---|---|
| 谢 | 谢 | 谢 | 谢 | 谢 | 谢 | xiè |
| 客 | 丶 | 宀 | 宀 | 客 | 客 | kè |
| 气 | 丿 | 仁 | 气 | 气 | 气 | qì |
| 吸 | 口 | 叨 | 吸 | 吸 | 吸 | xī |
| 烟 | 丶 | 丿 | 少 | 火 | 灯 | 烟 | 烟 |
| 烟 | 烟 | 烟 | 烟 | 烟 | 烟 | yān |

3. 把下列相同偏旁的汉字组成词语写在（  ）中：
Make up a word or phrase by combining each of the
following groups of characters that have one component in common with one of your own and put
what you have made in the brackets:

进（　　　　）　　　语（　　　　　　）
迎（　　　　）　　　请（　　　　　　）

你（　　　　）　　　国（　　　　　　）
什（　　　　）　　　图（　　　　　　）

4. 按正确笔顺临写下列汉字，注意笔画在田字格中的位置：

47

Copy each of the following characters in the correct stroke-order, paying attention to the position of each stroke in the crossed square:

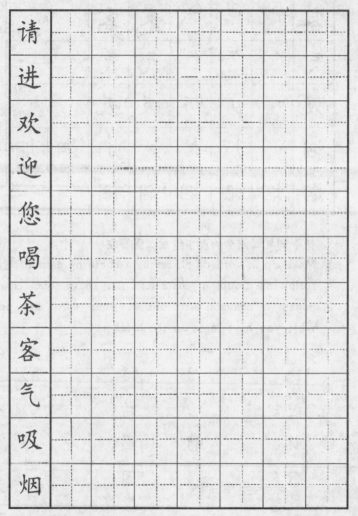

5. 把下列拼音写成汉字：

put the phonetic transcriptions in the following sentences into Chinese characters:

Nín _____ 好！

请 jìn _____ 。 Qǐng_____ 喝 chá _____ 。

Xièxie _____ 。

6. 给下列各组形近字注音并组成词语：

Put each of the following characters similar in shape and structure in each group into phonetic transcription, then make up a word or phrase with it and put what you have made in the brackets:

你____ (    )        她____ (    )
您____ (    )        地____ (    )

那____ (    )        吗____ (    )
哪____ (    )        妈____ (    )

49

# 第 九 课  Lesson 9

一、汉字分析

Analysis of Characters

1. 笔顺

Stroke-order

汉字笔顺基本规则（二）：先撇后捺。撇跟捺相交或相连，先写撇后写捺。例如：

Basic Stroke-order Rule(2): A left-falling stroke precedes a right-falling one. When the two cross each other or are linked in the same way, the left-falling one comes first. E.g.

人： ノ 人

由外到里。例如：

From outer strokes to inside ones. E.g.

习： 刁 习

问： 门 问

先外后里再封口。例如：

Outer strokes precede inside ones, and the sealing stroke comes last. E.g.

国： 冂 国 国

2. 汉字偏旁

Character component

院 { 阝 （左耳旁 zuǒěrpáng the left-hand component "阝"）
完

注意："左耳旁"和"右耳旁"所在的位置是不同的，如院、那。

Notice that the left-hand component "阝" and the right-hand component "阝" are different from each other in position. The former appears always to the left and the latter to the right, as in "院" and "那".

二、汉字练习

Character Exercises

1. 汉字认读：

Character recognition:

1）辨认下列汉字：

Identify the following characters in each of the following groups:

都　院　那

叫　喝　吗

姓　妈　她

2）认读词语：

Read out the following words and phrases:

51

学：学生　留学生

学习　学习什么　学习汉语

学院　外语学院

2. 按正确笔顺描写下列汉字：

Trace the following characters in the correct stroke-order:

| | | | | | |
|---|---|---|---|---|---|
| 问 | 门 | 问 | 问 | 问 | 问 | wèn |
| 留 | ⺍ | ⺥ | ⺳ | 留 | 留 | liú |
| 学 | 、 | 〟 | ⺌ | ⺍ | 业 | 学 学 |
| 学 | 学 | 学 | 学 | 学 | 学 | xué |
| 生 | ノ | ⺅ | 牛 | 生 | 生 | shēng |
| 贵 | 、 | 冂 | 口 | 中 | 虫 | 毒 毒 |
| 贵 | 贵 | 贵 | 贵 | 贵 | 贵 | guì |
| 姓 | 女 | 姓 | 姓 | 姓 | 姓 | xìng |
| 叫 | 口 | 叫 | 叫 | 叫 | 叫 | jiào |

| 外 | ノ | ク | 夕 | 列 | 外 | wài | |
|---|---|---|---|---|---|---|---|
| 院 | 卩 | 阝 | 阵 | 阼 | 陓 | 院 | 院 |
| 院 | 院 | 院 | 院 | 院 | 院 | yuàn | |
| 习 | 刁 | 刁 | 习 | 习 | 习 | xí | |

3. 临写下列汉字，注意笔画在田字格中的位置：

Copy each of the following characters, paying attention to the position of each stroke in the crossed square:

| 问 | | | | | | |
|---|---|---|---|---|---|---|
| 留 | | | | | | |
| 学 | | | | | | |
| 生 | | | | | | |
| 贵 | | | | | | |
| 姓 | | | | | | |

| 叫 | | | | | | | | |
|---|---|---|---|---|---|---|---|---|
| 外 | | | | | | | | |
| 院 | | | | | | | | |
| 习 | | | | | | | | |

4. 给下列各组汉字注音，把相同的偏旁写在（　）中：
Write each of the following characters in phonetic transcription and put the component the characters in each group have in common in the brackets:

姓____ 妈____ 她____ 好____（　　）

叫____ 喝____ 吗____ 呢____ 哪____

（　　）

请____ 语____ 谢____ 谁____（　　）

5. 把下列拼音写成汉字：
Put the following phonetic transcriptions into Chinese characters to make up words or phrases with the given characters:

54

学 { xí _____  
    sheng _____  
    yuàn _____ }

请 { wèn _____  
    jìn _____  
    hē _____ 茶  
    kàn _____ 书 }

# 第 十 课　Lesson 10

一、汉字分析

Analysis of Characters

1. 笔顺

Stroke-order

汉字笔顺基本规则(三)：从左到右。例如：

Basic Stroke-order Rule (3): From left strokes to right. E.g.

儿：丿　儿

住：亻　住

2. 汉字偏旁

Character component

宿 { 宀
　 佰

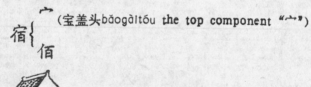

（宝盖头 bǎogàitóu the top component "宀"）

宀 古字象房屋的形状。

The top component "宀" originated from the ancient ideogram "∧" symbolizing a house.

"宿"是古"宿"字，表示人在屋里住宿。

The character "宿" originated from the ideogram "宿" symbolizing a house with a person under its roof.

二、汉字练习

Character Exercises

1. 、汉字认读：

Character recognition:

1）辨认下列汉字：

Identify characters in each of the following pairs:

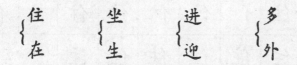

$$\left\{\begin{matrix}住\\在\end{matrix}\right. \quad \left\{\begin{matrix}坐\\生\end{matrix}\right. \quad \left\{\begin{matrix}进\\迎\end{matrix}\right. \quad \left\{\begin{matrix}多\\外\end{matrix}\right.$$

2）认读下列句子：

Read out the following sentences:

请问，王大夫在吗？

不在，她在五三四号。

2. 按正确笔顺描写下列汉字：

Trace the following characters in the correct stroke-order:

| 在 | 一 | ナ | ナ | 右 | 存 | 在 | 在 |
|---|---|---|---|---|---|---|---|
| 在 | 在 | 在 | 在 | 在 | 在 | zài | |
| 坐 | 人 | 纵 | 坐 | 坐 | 坐 | zuò | |
| 儿 | 丿 | 儿 | 儿 | 儿 | 儿 | ér | |
| 宿 | 宀 | 宀 | 宁 | 宿 | 宿 | sù | |
| 舍 | 人 | 人 | 人 | 全 | 舍 | shè | |
| 住 | 亻 | 亻 | 广 | 仁 | 住 | 住 | 住 |
| 住 | 住 | 住 | 住 | 住 | 住 | zhù | |
| 多 | 夕 | 多 | 多 | 多 | 多 | duō | |
| 少 | 小 | 少 | 少 | 少 | 少 | shǎo | |
| 号 | 口 | 卫 | 号 | 号 | 号 | hào | |
| 四 | 丨 | 冂 | 四 | 四 | 四 | sì | |
| 层 | 尸 | 尸 | 尼 | 层 | 层 | céng | |

| | | | | | | |
|---|---|---|---|---|---|---|
| 二 | 二 | 二 | 二 | 二 | 二 | èr |
| 三 | 三 | 三 | 三 | 三 | 三 | sān |
| 一 | 一 | 一 | 一 | 一 | 一 | yī |
| 五 | 五 | 五 | 五 | 五 | 五 | wǔ |

3．临写下列汉字，注意汉字的笔顺：

Copy the following characters, paying special attention to their proper stroke-order:

| | | | | | | | |
|---|---|---|---|---|---|---|---|
| 在 | | | | | | | |
| 宿 | | | | | | | |
| 舍 | | | | | | | |
| 住 | | | | | | | |
| 多 | | | | | | | |
| 少 | | | | | | | |
| 号 | | | | | | | |

4. 给下列各组汉字注音，把相同的偏旁写在（ ）中：
Write each of the following characters in phonetic
transcription and put in the brackets the component
that the characters in each group have in common:

坐＿＿＿ 地＿＿＿ 在＿＿＿（　　　　　）

住＿＿＿ 你＿＿＿ 他＿＿＿（　　　　　）

多＿＿＿ 外＿＿＿　　　　　（　　　　　）

5. 把下列词语中的拼音写成汉字：
Write out the characters that the phonetic transcriptions in the following words and phrases represent:

宿 shè＿＿＿＿ 请 zuò＿＿＿＿ duō＿＿＿＿少

不 zài＿＿＿＿ zhù＿＿＿＿哪儿 请 jìn＿＿＿＿

6. 把下列阿拉伯数字写成汉字：
Give the Chinese equivalents of the following Arabic
figures:

1＿＿＿＿2＿＿＿＿3＿＿＿＿4＿＿＿＿5＿＿＿＿

她住多少号？

她住435＿＿＿＿＿＿＿＿号。

# 第十一课　Lesson 11

## 一、汉字分析
Analysis of Characters

### 1. 笔顺
Stroke-order

汉字笔顺规则（四）：先横后竖。横和竖相交，一般先写横。例如：

Basic Stroke-order Rule (4): A horizontal stroke precedes a vertical one. When a horizontal stroke crosses with a vertical one, the former comes first.

十：　一　十

### 2. 汉字偏旁
Character component

现{王（王字旁 wángzìpáng the component "王"）
　　见

## 二、汉字练习
Character Exercises

### 1. 汉字认读：
Character recognition:

1) 认读词语：
Read out the following words and phrases:

一下儿　　用一下儿　看一下儿

坐一下儿

中国画报　汉语词典　汉语书

2) 认读电话号码：
Read out the following telephone numbers:

五五·六七八九

二七·七五三一

3) 认读句子：
Read out the following sentences:

他用汉语词典。　　你看中国画报。

我学习汉语。

2. 按笔顺写出下列汉字的笔画：
Write out the strokes in each of the following
characters in the correct stroke-order:

例字：
Example:

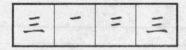

| | | | | | | | |
|---|---|---|---|---|---|---|---|
| 坐 | | | | | | | |
| 住 | | | | | | | |
| 宿 | | | | | | | |
| 多 | | | | | | | |
| 舍 | | | | | | | |
| 号 | | | | | | | |

3. 按正确笔顺描写下列汉字：

Trace the following characters in the correct stroke-order:

| | | | | | | |
|---|---|---|---|---|---|---|
| 还 | 不 | 还 | 还 | 还 | 还 | huán |
| 画 | 一 | 囬 | 画 | 画 | 画 | huà |
| 报 | 一 | 十 | 扌 | 扩 | 扩 | 报 报 |
| 报 | 报 | 报 | 报 | 报 | 报 | bào |
| 词 | 讠 | 讠 | 讠 | 词 | 词 | cí |

| 典 | 丶 | 冂 | 冂 | 冉 | 曲 | 曲 | 典 |
| 典 | 典 | 典 | 典 | 典 | 典 | diǎn | |
| 再 | 一 | 厂 | 冂 | 币 | 丙 | 再 | 再 |
| 再 | 再 | 再 | 再 | 再 | 再 | zài | |
| 见 | 丨 | 冂 | 贝 | 见 | 见 | jiàn | |
| 现 | 一 | 二 | 王 | 王 | 现 | xiàn | |
| 用 | 丿 | 冂 | 月 | 月 | 用 | yòng | |
| 下 | 一 | 丁 | 下 | 下 | 下 | xià | |
| 六 | 亠 | 六 | 六 | 六 | 六 | liù | |
| 七 | 一 | 七 | 七 | 七 | 七 | qī | |
| 八 | 丿 | 八 | 八 | 八 | 八 | bā | |
| 九 | 丿 | 九 | 九 | 九 | 九 | jiǔ | |
| 十 | 一 | 十 | 十 | 十 | 十 | shí | |

4. 临写下列汉字：

Copy the following characters:

| 还 | | | | | | | | |
|---|---|---|---|---|---|---|---|---|
| 画 | 一 | | | | | | | |
| 报 | | | | | | | | |
| 词 | | | | | | | | |
| 典 | | | | | | | | |
| 再 | | | | | | | | |
| 见 | | | | | | | | |
| 现 | | | | | | | | |
| 用 | | | | | | | | |
| 下 | | | | | | | | |
| 九 | | | | | | | | |

5. 给下列各组汉字注音，把相同的偏旁写在（　）中：

Write each of the following characters in phonetic transcription and put in the brackets the component that the characters in each group have in common:

词＿＿＿　语＿＿＿　请＿＿＿　谢＿＿＿　谁＿＿＿

（　　　）

还＿＿＿　迎＿＿＿　进＿＿＿　这＿＿＿　（　　　）

6. 把下列词语中的拼音写成汉字：

Put the phonetic transcriptions in the following words and phrases into Chinese characters:

词 diǎn ＿＿＿＿　汉 yǔ ＿＿＿＿　huà ＿＿＿＿报

现 zài ＿＿＿＿　zài ＿＿＿＿见　请 zuò ＿＿＿＿

学 xí ＿＿＿＿　xué ＿＿＿＿习　再 xuéxí ＿＿＿＿

# 第十二课　Lesson 12

一、汉字分析

Analysis of Characters

笔顺

Stroke-order

汉字笔顺的基本规则归纳如下：

Following is a summary of the basic stroke-order of rules of Chinese characters:

| 例　　字<br>Examples | 笔　　顺<br>Stroke-order | 规　　　　则<br>Rules |
|---|---|---|
| 十 | 一　十 | 先横后竖<br>A horizontal stroke preceding a vertical one |
| 人 | ノ　人 | 先撇后捺<br>A left-falling stroke preceding a right-falling one |
| 三 | 一　二　三 | 从上到下<br>From top stroke to bottom one |
| 儿 | ノ　儿 | 从左到右<br>From left stroke to right one |

| | | |
|---|---|---|
| 问 | 门 问 | 从外到里<br>From outer strokes to inside ones |
| 国 | 冂 国 国 | 先外后里再封口<br>Outer strokes preceding inside ones, and the sealing stroke coming last |
| 小<br>xiǎo | 亅 小 小 | 先中间后两边<br>Middle stroke preceding the strokes on both sides |

二、汉字练习

Character Exercises

1. 汉字认读：

Character recognition:

1) 认读词语：

Read out the following words and phrases:

女：女朋友　女学生　女老师

女大夫

语：汉语　英语　外语

2) 认读下列各偏旁的汉字：

Read out the characters in each of the following groups having one component in common:

亻（立人旁）：你　他　们　住　什

女（女字旁）：她　妈　好　姓

68

口（口字旁）：喝　叫　吗　呢　哪

讠（言字旁）：语　词　请　谢　谁

认　识

辶（走之旁）：迎　进　还　这

扌（土字旁）：地　坐　在　去

阝（右耳旁）：都　那

阝（左耳旁）：院

艹（草字头）：茶　英

宀（宝盖头）：宿

目（目字底）：看

王（王字旁）：现

囗（国字框）：国　图

**2.** 按正确笔顺写出下列汉字的笔画：
Write out the strokes in each of the following characters in the correct stroke-order:

| 请 | | | | | | | |
|---|---|---|---|---|---|---|---|
| 问 | | | | | | | |
| 您 | | | | | | | |
| 是 | | | | | | | |
| 法 | | | | | | | |
| 国 | | | | | | | |
| 人 | | | | | | | |
| 吗 | | | | | | | |

3. 按正确笔顺描写下列汉字：

Trace the following characters in the correct stroke-order:

| 认 | 讠 | 认 | 认 | 认 | 认 | rèn |
|---|---|---|---|---|---|---|
| 识 | 讠 | 识 | 识 | 识 | 识 | shí |
| 先 | 丿 | 𠂉 | 牛 | 生 | 先 | xiān |

| | | | | | | |
|---|---|---|---|---|---|---|
| 女 | 女 | 女 | 女 | 女 | 女 | nǚ |
| 英 | 艹 | 艹 | 苎 | 苎 | 英 | 英 |
| 英 | 英 | 英 | 英 | 英 | 英 | yīng |
| 法 | 丶 | 冫 | 氵 | 泫 | 法 | 法 |
| 法 | 法 | 法 | 法 | 法 | 法 | fǎ |
| 常 | 丶 | 丷 | 丷 | 丷 | 尚 | 堂 |
| 常 | 常 | 常 | 常 | 常 | 常 | cháng |
| 去 | 去 | 去 | 去 | 去 | 去 | qù |

**4.** 临写下列汉字，注意笔画在田字格中的位置：

Copy each of the following characters, paying attention to the position of each stroke in the crossed square:

| | | | | | | | |
|---|---|---|---|---|---|---|---|
| 女 | | | | | | | |
| 先 | | | | | | | |

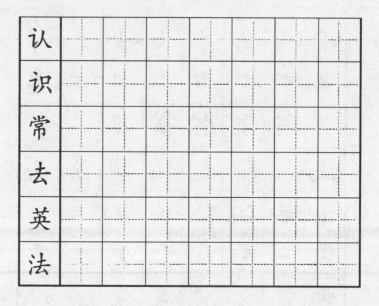

| 认 | | | | | | | | |
| 识 | | | | | | | | |
| 常 | | | | | | | | |
| 去 | | | | | | | | |
| 英 | | | | | | | | |
| 法 | | | | | | | | |

5. 给下列汉字注音并组成词语：

Write each of the following characters in phonetic transcription, then make up a word or phrase with each by adding another character to it and put what you have made in the brackets:

例字：
Example:

语 ___yǔ___ （汉语）

词 ___cí___ （词典）

进 _____ （    ）        国 _____ （     ）

迎 _____ （    ）        图 _____ （     ）

$$\left\{\begin{array}{l}\text{朋}\underline{\qquad}(\quad)\\[2mm]\text{用}\underline{\qquad}(\quad)\end{array}\right.\qquad\left\{\begin{array}{l}\text{住}\underline{\qquad}(\quad)\\[2mm]\text{在}\underline{\qquad}(\quad)\end{array}\right.$$

$$\left\{\begin{array}{l}\text{地}\underline{\qquad}(\quad)\\[2mm]\text{他}\underline{\qquad}(\quad)\end{array}\right.\qquad\left\{\begin{array}{l}\text{妈}\underline{\qquad}(\quad)\\[2mm]\text{吗}\underline{\qquad}(\quad)\end{array}\right.$$

**6.** 把下列词语中的拼音写成汉字：

Put the phonetic transcriptions in the following words and phrases into Chinese characters:

$$\left\{\begin{array}{l}\text{zài}\underline{\qquad}\text{见}\\[2mm]\text{现 zài}\underline{\qquad}\end{array}\right.\qquad\left\{\begin{array}{l}\text{dì}\underline{\qquad}\text{弟}\\[2mm]\text{dì}\underline{\qquad}\text{图}\end{array}\right.$$

$$\left\{\begin{array}{l}\text{rèn}\underline{\qquad}\text{识}\\[2mm]\text{中国 rén}\underline{\qquad}\end{array}\right.\qquad\left\{\begin{array}{l}\text{huān}\underline{\qquad}\text{迎}\\[2mm]\text{huán}\underline{\qquad}\text{书}\end{array}\right.$$

**7.** 找出下列句子中的错字并改正：

Pick out the wrongly written characters in the following sentences, then give the correct forms in the brackets:

请喈茶。（　　　）

你佳多少号？（　　　）（　　　）

她常去学生宿舍。（　　　）（　　　）

（　　　）

8. 按照下面的偏旁各写出四个汉字：
   Write four different characters in the blanks in each
   group, all containing the component given at the
   head:

   亻 _____  _____  _____  _____

   女 _____  _____  _____  _____

   口 _____  _____  _____  _____

   讠 _____  _____  _____  _____

   辶 _____  _____  _____  _____

   扌 _____  _____  _____  _____

# 第十三课　Lesson 13

一、汉字分析

Analysis of Characters

1. 合体字的书写顺序

The order of component parts for writing compound characters

汉字绝大部分是合体字。合体字的基本结构有三种：上下结构、左右结构和内外结构。现用示意图表示不同类型的结构，图中数字表示笔顺的先后。

Most Chinese characters are compound forms composed of two or three component parts, which fall into three main types of arrangement: (1) one component part on top of the other, (2) two component parts placed side by side, (3) one component part enclosed in the other.

Following are a number of diagrams showing the above-mentioned three types of arrangement. The numerals in the diagrams indicate the order for the writing of the component parts of a compound character.

上下结构：

One component part on top of the other:

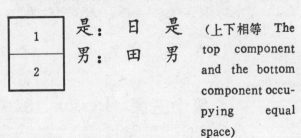

是：日 是　（上下相等 The top component and the bottom component occupying equal space)

男：田 男

字：宀 字　（上小下大 The top component occupying less space than the bottom component

宿：宀 疒 宿

典：曲 典　（上大下小 The top component occupying more space than the bottom component)

您：亻 你 您

## 2．汉字偏旁
Character components

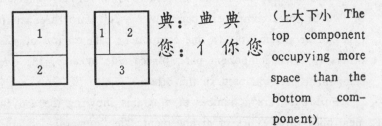

笔 { 竹 （竹字头 zhúzìtóu the top component "竹"）
　　毛

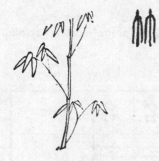

竹（⺮）古字象竹叶。

The component "⺮" is a variant of the character "竹" which
came from the ancient ideogram on the left symbolizing
bamboo leaves.

制作毛笔需用竹子，所以"笔"是竹字头。

Chinese writing brushes are usually made of a fine
bamboo pole as the shaft and a tuft of hair fixed at one
end of the shaft as the brush. That is why the character
"笔" contains the component "⺮".

店 { 广 （广字头 guǎngzìtóu the component "广"）
shop 占

广　　　　　广古"广"字象屋形，"店"是屋子，
用"广"字头。

The component "广" originated from the ideogram "广"
symbolizing a house or room. The character "店" means
"shop", a building where goods are sold, which accounts
for the "广" component in the character.

二、汉字练习
Character Exercises

1. 按正确笔顺描写下列汉字：
   Trace the following characters in the correct stroke-order:

| | | | | | | |
|---|---|---|---|---|---|---|
| 名 | 名 | 名 | 名 | 名 | 名 | míng |
| 字 | 字 | 字 | 字 | 字 | 字 | zì |
| 喂 | 喂 | 喂 | 喂 | 喂 | 喂 | wèi |
| 啊 | 啊 | 啊 | 啊 | 啊 | 啊 | ā |
| 商 | 商 | 商 | 商 | 商 | 商 | shāng |
| 店 | 店 | 店 | 店 | 店 | 店 | diàn |
| 买 | 买 | 买 | 买 | 买 | 买 | mǎi |
| 笔 | 笔 | 笔 | 笔 | 笔 | 笔 | bǐ |
| 来 | 来 | 来 | 来 | 来 | 来 | lái |
| 介 | 介 | 介 | 介 | 介 | 介 | jiè |
| 绍 | 绍 | 绍 | 绍 | 绍 | 绍 | shào |

| | | | | | | |
|---|---|---|---|---|---|---|
| 男 | 男 | 男 | 男 | 男 | 男 | nán |
| 对 | 对 | 对 | 对 | 对 | 对 | duì |
| 和 | 和 | 和 | 和 | 和 | 和 | hé |
| 说 | 说 | 说 | 说 | 说 | 说 | shuō |

2. 按正确笔顺临写下列汉字：

Copy the following characters in the correct stroke-order:

| 名 | | | | | | | |
|---|---|---|---|---|---|---|---|
| 字 | | | | | | | |
| 买 | | | | | | | |
| 笔 | | | | | | | |
| 来 | | | | | | | |
| 商 | | | | | | | |
| 店 | | | | | | | |

| 男 | | | | | | | |
|---|---|---|---|---|---|---|---|
| 对 | | | | | | | |
| 和 | | | | | | | |
| 说 | | | | | | | |

3. 分析下列汉字的结构，并把它填入结构示意图后 的 方格中：

Analyze the arrangement of the component parts of each of the following characters and write the characters in the squares in the manner indicated by the diagrams given at the head:

名　买　笔　介　留　学　常

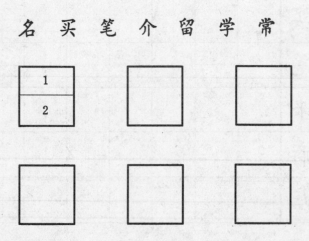

4. 给下列各组汉字注音，把相同的偏旁写在（ ）中：
   Transcribe the following characters and put in the brackets the component that the characters in each group have in common:

喂_____ 啊_____ 呢_____ 吗_____

哪_____ 喝_____ 叫_____ （　　）

说_____ 语_____ 请_____ 谢_____

认_____ 识_____ 谁_____ （　　）

字_____ 宿_____ （　　）

5. 把下列词语中的拼音写成汉字：
   Put the phonetic transcription in each of the following words and phrases into a Chinese character:

中 guó_____  介 shào_____  shāng_____ 店

mǎi_____ 笔  míng_____ 字  Hàn_____ 字

xué_____ 习  汉 yǔ_____  rèn_____ 识

81

# 第十四课　Lesson 14

一、汉字分析
Analysis of Characters

1. 合体字的书写顺序
The order of component parts for writing compound characters

左右结构（一）：
Two component parts placed side by side (1):

朋：月　朋　（左右相等
(friend)　The left-hand and right-hand components occupying equal space)

信：亻　信　（左小右大
The left-hand component occupying less space than the right-hand one)

都：者　都　（左大右小
The left-hand component occupying more space than the right-hand one)

**2. 汉字偏旁**

Character component

$$想\begin{cases}相\\心\end{cases}$$

心（心字底 xīnzìdǐ the bottom component "心"）

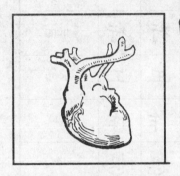

心　古字象心的形状。

The bottom component "心" originated from the ideogram on the left symbolizing the heart,

古人认为"心"是管思想的，所以"想"字用"心"字底。

The ancients regarded the human heart as the organ of thinking, which accouts for the "心" component in the character "想".

$$银\begin{cases}钅\\艮\end{cases}$$

(silver)

（金字旁 jīnzìpáng the component "钅"）

金字旁的字跟金属物有关，如"银"。

The meaning of any character containing the component "钅" mostly has something to do with metal, e.g. "银".

**二、汉字练习**

Character Exercises

1. 按正确笔顺描写下列汉字:
   Trace the following characters in the correct stroke-order:

| | | | | | | |
|---|---|---|---|---|---|---|
| 银 | 银 | 银 | 银 | 银 | 银 | yín |
| 行 | 行 | 行 | 行 | 行 | 行 | háng |
| 工 | 工 | 工 | 工 | 工 | 工 | gōng |
| 作 | 作 | 作 | 作 | 作 | 作 | zuò |
| 想 | 想 | 想 | 想 | 想 | 想 | xiǎng |
| 家 | 家 | 家 | 家 | 家 | 家 | jiā |
| 没 | 没 | 没 | 没 | 没 | 没 | méi |
| 有 | 有 | 有 | 有 | 有 | 有 | yǒu |
| 姐 | 姐 | 姐 | 姐 | 姐 | 姐 | jiě |
| 妹 | 妹 | 妹 | 妹 | 妹 | 妹 | mèi |
| 爱 | 爱 | 爱 | 爱 | 爱 | 爱 | ài |

| | | | | | | |
|---|---|---|---|---|---|---|
| 孩 | 孩 | 孩 | 孩 | 孩 | 孩 | hái |
| 子 | 子 | 子 | 子 | 子 | 子 | zǐ |
| 告 | 告 | 告 | 告 | 告 | 告 | gào |
| 诉 | 诉 | 诉 | 诉 | 诉 | 诉 | sù |
| 给 | 给 | 给 | 给 | 给 | 给 | gěi |
| 写 | 写 | 写 | 写 | 写 | 写 | xiě |
| 信 | 信 | 信 | 信 | 信 | 信 | xìn |

2. 按正确笔顺临写下列汉字:

Copy the following characters in the following characters in the correct stroke-order:

| | | | | | | | |
|---|---|---|---|---|---|---|---|
| 银 | | | | | | | |
| 行 | | | | | | | |
| 工 | | | | | | | |
| 作 | | | | | | | |

| 想 | | | | | | | |
|---|---|---|---|---|---|---|---|
| 家 | | | | | | | |
| 没 | | | | | | | |
| 有 | | | | | | | |
| 姐 | | | | | | | |
| 妹 | | | | | | | |
| 爱 | | | | | | | |
| 孩 | | | | | | | |
| 子 | | | | | | | |
| 告 | | | | | | | |
| 诉 | | | | | | | |
| 给 | | | | | | | |

3. 分析下列汉字的结构，并把它填入结构示意图后 的 方格中：

Analyze the arrangement of the component parts of each of the following characters and write the characters in the squares in the manner shown in the diagrams given on the left:

新　作　没　妹　姐　银　行　孩
给　诉

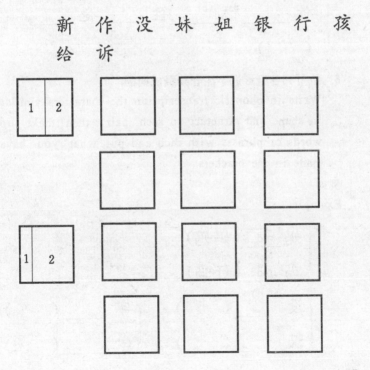

4. 给下列各组汉字注音，把相同的偏旁写在（　）中：

Write each of the following characters in phonetic transcription and put in the brackets the component that the characters in each group have in common:

想_____您_____（　　　）

家_____宿_____字_____（　　　）

妈_____姐_____妹_____她_____

（　　　）

作_____信_____住_____他_____

（　　　）

5. 给下列各组形近字注音并组成词语：

Write in phonetic transcription the characters similar in shape and structure in each pair, then make up words or phrases with each and put what you have made in the brackets:

例如：

Example:

$\left\{\begin{array}{l}\text{妈 }\underline{\text{mā}}\text{（妈妈）}\\ \text{吗 }\underline{\text{ma}}\text{（好吗）}\end{array}\right.$

$\left\{\begin{array}{l}\text{没_____（　　　）}\\ \text{汉_____（　　　）}\end{array}\right.$ $\left\{\begin{array}{l}\text{字_____（　　　）}\\ \text{学_____（　　　）}\end{array}\right.$

88

$$\begin{cases} 很 \underline{\hspace{2cm}} (\quad) \\ 银 \underline{\hspace{2cm}} (\quad) \end{cases} \qquad \begin{cases} 地 \underline{\hspace{2cm}} (\quad) \\ 他 \underline{\hspace{2cm}} (\quad) \end{cases}$$

$$\begin{cases} 友 \underline{\hspace{2cm}} (\quad) \\ 有 \underline{\hspace{2cm}} (\quad) \end{cases} \qquad \begin{cases} 作 \underline{\hspace{2cm}} (\quad) \\ 什 \underline{\hspace{2cm}} (\quad) \end{cases}$$

6. 猜字谜:

Guess the riddle about a Chinese character:

"他" 没有人,

"地" 没有土 (tǔ)。

(猜一汉字,答案见下课。The solution to the riddle is a
　　　　　　　Chinese character, given in
　　　　　　　Lesson 15.)

# 第十五课　Lesson 15

## 一、汉字分析
### Analysis of Characters

1. 合体字书写顺序

The order of component parts for writing compound characters:

左右结构（二）：

Two component parts placed side by side (2):

语：讠　语　语　（左小右大 The left-hand component occupying less space than the right-hand one）

教：耂　孝　教　（左大右小 The left-hand component occupying more space than the right-hand one）

2. 汉字偏旁

Character component

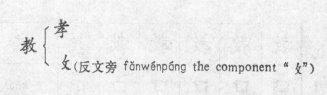

教 { 孝

攵（反文旁 fǎnwénpáng the component "攵"）

攴　攵　　古字象手形。用反文旁的字大都与手
的活动有关。

The component "攵" came from "攴", a variant of the
above ancient ideogram symbolizing a hand. Therefore,
characters containing "攵" usually have a connotation
pertaining to the hand or its functions.

二、汉字练习

Character Exercises

1. 按正确笔顺描写下列汉字：

Trace the following characters in the corret stroke-
order:

| | | | | | | |
|---|---|---|---|---|---|---|
| 中 | 中 | 中 | 中 | 中 | 中 | zhōng |
| 文 | 文 | 文 | 文 | 文 | 文 | wén |
| 系 | 系 | 系 | 系 | 系 | 系 | xì |
| 个 | 个 | 个 | 个 | 个 | 个 | gè |
| 几 | 几 | 几 | 几 | 几 | 几 | jǐ |

| | | | | | | |
|---|---|---|---|---|---|---|
| 教 | 教 | 教 | 教 | 教 | 教 | jiāo |
| 口 | 口 | 口 | 口 | 口 | 口 | kǒu |
| 敢 | 敢 | 敢 | 敢 | 敢 | 敢 | gǎn |
| 当 | 当 | 当 | 当 | 当 | 当 | dāng |
| 互 | 互 | 互 | 互 | 互 | 互 | hù |
| 相 | 相 | 相 | 相 | 相 | 相 | xiāng |
| 新 | 新 | 新 | 新 | 新 | 新 | xīn |
| 阅 | 阅 | 阅 | 阅 | 阅 | 阅 | yuè |
| 览 | 览 | 览 | 览 | 览 | 览 | lǎn |
| 室 | 室 | 室 | 室 | 室 | 室 | shì |
| 杂 | 杂 | 杂 | 杂 | 杂 | 杂 | zá |
| 志 | 志 | 志 | 志 | 志 | 志 | zhì |
| 本 | 本 | 本 | 本 | 本 | 本 | běn |

| 馆 | 馆 | 馆 | 馆 | 馆 | 馆 | guǎn |

2. 按正确笔顺临写下列汉字：

Copy the following characters in the correct stroke-order:

| 中 | | | | | | | |
|---|---|---|---|---|---|---|---|
| 文 | | | | | | | |
| 系 | | | | | | | |
| 个 | | | | | | | |
| 几 | | | | | | | |
| 教 | | | | | | | |
| 口 | | | | | | | |
| 敢 | | | | | | | |
| 当 | | | | | | | |
| 互 | | | | | | | |

| 相 | | | | | | | |
|---|---|---|---|---|---|---|---|
| 新 | | | | | | | |
| 阅 | | | | | | | |
| 览 | | | | | | | |
| 室 | | | | | | | |
| 杂 | | | | | | | |
| 志 | | | | | | | |
| 本 | | | | | | | |
| 馆 | | | | | | | |

3. 分析下列汉字的结构，把它填入结构示意图后的方格中：

Analyze the arrangement of the component parts of each of the following characters and write the characters in the squares in the manner shown in the diagrams given on the left:

馆　敢　新　语　报　院

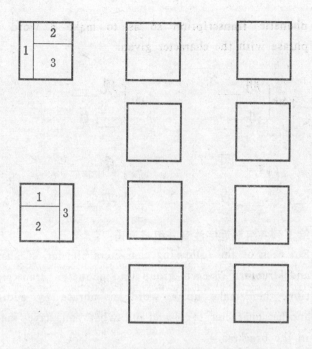

4. 给下列各组汉字注音，把相同的偏旁写在（ ）中：
Write each of the following characters in phonetic transcription and put in the brackets the component that the characters in each group have in common:

教_____ 敢_____（　　）

室_____ 家_____ 宿_____（　　）

志_____ 想_____ 您_____（　　）

5. 根据拼音写出汉字：
Fill in each blank with a character according to the

phonetic transcription so as to make a word **or** phrase with the character given:

yǒu { 朋 ___
     { 没 ___

zài { 现 ___
     { ___ 见

dì { ___ 图
    { ___ 弟

zuò { 请 ___
     { 工 ___

6. 给下列各组形近字注音并组成词语：

Put each of the following characters similar in shape and structure in each group into phonetic transcription, then make up a word or phrase by adding another character to it and put what you have made in the brackets:

{ 儿 _____ ( )
{ 几 _____ ( )

{ 人 _____ ( )
{ 八 _____ ( )

{ 个 _____ ( )
{ 介 _____ ( )

{ 教 _____ ( )
{ 敢 _____ ( )

（上一课字谜是"也"字。

The solution to the riddle in Lesson 14 is the character "也"。）

# 第十六课　Lesson 16

一、汉字分析

Analysis of Characters

1. 合体字的书写顺序

The order of component parts for writing compound characters:

左右结构（三）：

Component parts placed side by side (3):

 谢：讠　诮　谢　　（左中右相等

The left-hand,

the middle and the right-hand components

occupying equal space）

2. 汉字偏旁

Character component

 （衣字旁 yīzìpáng the component "衣"）

 衣（衤）古字象衣形。

The component "衤" is

a variant of the char-

acter "衣" which developed from the above

ideogram symbolizing a shirt or blouse.

衣字旁的字大都与服装有关，如"裙子"、"衬衫"。

Therefore, characters containing "衤" usually

refer to or have something to do with clothing, e.g.

"裙子"、"衬衫".

二、汉字练习

Character Exercises

1. 按正确笔顺描写下列汉字：

Trace the following characters in the correct stroke-

order:

| | | | | | | |
|---|---|---|---|---|---|---|
| 条 | 条 | 条 | 条 | 条 | 条 | tiáo |
| 裙 | 裙 | 裙 | 裙 | 裙 | 裙 | qún |
| 两 | 两 | 两 | 两 | 两 | 两 | liǎng |
| 张 | 张 | 张 | 张 | 张 | 张 | zhāng |
| 票 | 票 | 票 | 票 | 票 | 票 | piào |
| 京 | 京 | 京 | 京 | 京 | 京 | jīng |
| 剧 | 剧 | 剧 | 剧 | 剧 | 剧 | jù |
| 晚 | 晚 | 晚 | 晚 | 晚 | 晚 | wǎn |
| 上 | 上 | 上 | 上 | 上 | 上 | shàng |

| | | | | | | |
|---|---|---|---|---|---|---|
| 太 | 太 | 太 | 太 | 太 | 太 | tài |
| 从 | 从 | 从 | 从 | 从 | 从 | cóng |
| 找 | 找 | 找 | 找 | 找 | 找 | zhǎo |
| 旧 | 旧 | 旧 | 旧 | 旧 | 旧 | jiù |
| 穿 | 穿 | 穿 | 穿 | 穿 | 穿 | chuān |
| 件 | 件 | 件 | 件 | 件 | 件 | jiàn |
| 衬 | 衬 | 衬 | 衬 | 衬 | 衬 | chèn |
| 衫 | 衫 | 衫 | 衫 | 衫 | 衫 | shān |
| 绿 | 绿 | 绿 | 绿 | 绿 | 绿 | lǜ |
| 白 | 白 | 白 | 白 | 白 | 白 | bái |

2. 按正确笔顺临写下列汉字：
Copy the following characters in the correct stroke-order:

| 条 | | | | | | | | | |
|---|---|---|---|---|---|---|---|---|---|
| | | | | | | | | | |

裙

两

张

票

京

剧

晚

上

太

从

找

旧

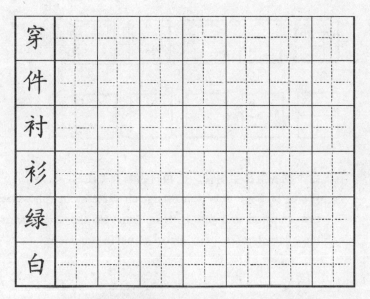

| 穿 | | | | | | | | |
| --- | --- | --- | --- | --- | --- | --- | --- | --- |
| 件 | | | | | | | | |
| 衬 | | | | | | | | |
| 衫 | | | | | | | | |
| 绿 | | | | | | | | |
| 白 | | | | | | | | |

3. 分析下列汉字的结构，把它填入结构示意图后的方格中：
Analyze the arrangement of the component parts of each of the following characters and write the characters in the squares in the manner shown in the diagrams given on the left:

哪　张　票　晚　找　条　裙　旧

穿　件　绿　衬　衫　剧

|   |   |   |   |   |
|---|---|---|---|---|
| 1 | 2 |   |   |   |

|   |   |   |   |   |
|---|---|---|---|---|
| 1 |   |   |   |   |
| 2 |   |   |   |   |

4. 给下列各组汉字注音，把相同的偏旁写在（ ）中：

Write each of the following characters in phonetic transcription and put in the brackets the component the characters in each group have in common:

裙＿＿＿＿ 衬＿＿＿＿ 衫＿＿＿＿ （ ）

绿＿＿＿＿ 给＿＿＿＿ 绍＿＿＿＿ （ ）

件＿＿＿＿ 什＿＿＿＿ 作＿＿＿＿ （ ）

5. 给下列各组形近字注音并组成词语：

Put each of the followiug characters similar in shape and structure in each group into phonetic transcription, then make up a word or phrase by adding another character to it and put what you have made in the parenthesis:

⎧ 我＿＿＿＿（ ）　⎧ 大＿＿＿＿（ ）
⎨
⎩ 找＿＿＿＿（ ）　⎩ 太＿＿＿＿（ ）

$\left\{\begin{array}{l}给 \underline{\qquad}（\quad）\\ 绍 \underline{\qquad}（\quad）\end{array}\right.$  $\left\{\begin{array}{l}条 \underline{\qquad}（\quad）\\ 杂 \underline{\qquad}（\quad）\end{array}\right.$

6. 根据拼音写出汉字：

Fill in each blank with a character according to the phonetic transcription so as to make a word or phrase with the character given:

qún \underline{\qquad}子    hái \underline{\qquad}子

xīn \underline{\qquad}的    jiù \underline{\qquad}的

nán \underline{\qquad}的    nǚ \underline{\qquad}的

lù \underline{\qquad}的    bái \underline{\qquad}的

7. 写出量词：

Fill in each blank with an appropriate measure word:

五\underline{\qquad}系        两\underline{\qquad}票

三\underline{\qquad}杂志     七\underline{\qquad}词典

十二\underline{\qquad}老师    九十八\underline{\qquad}学生

# 第十七课 Lesson 17

一、汉字分析
Analysis of Characters
汉字偏旁
Character components

刻 {亥
{ 刂（立刀旁 lìdāopáng the component " 刂"）

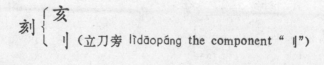

刀（刂）古字象把刀。
The component " 刂" is a variant of the character "刀" which originated from the ideogram on the lefe symbolizing a knife.

立刀旁的字大都与刀的名称和动作有关。如"刻"，本意是用刀雕刻。

That is why the meaning of any characters containing " 刂" has something to do with a knife in most cases. The character "刻", for example, means "to carve with a carving tool".

104

起 ｛ 走（走字旁 zǒuzìpáng the component "走"）
己

 走 这个古字上边 "大" 象人两手摆动走路。

下边 "止" 就是脚，表示行动。

The component "走" came from the above ancient ideogram which is composed of "大", symbolizine a person swinging his arms while walking, and "止", symbolizing his feet.

二、汉字练习

Character Exercises

1. 按正确笔顺描写下列汉字：

Trace the following characters in the correct stoke-order:

| | | | | | | |
|---|---|---|---|---|---|---|
| 点 | 点 | 点 | 点 | 点 | 点 | diǎn |
| 食 | 食 | 食 | 食 | 食 | 食 | shí |
| 堂 | 堂 | 堂 | 堂 | 堂 | 堂 | táng |
| 差 | 差 | 差 | 差 | 差 | 差 | chà |
| 分 | 分 | 分 | 分 | 分 | 分 | fēn |

| | | | | | | |
|---|---|---|---|---|---|---|
| 刻 | 刻 | 刻 | 刻 | 刻 | 刻 | kè |
| 课 | 课 | 课 | 课 | 课 | 课 | kè |
| 以 | 以 | 以 | 以 | 以 | 以 | yǐ |
| 后 | 后 | 后 | 后 | 后 | 后 | hòu |
| 事 | 事 | 事 | 事 | 事 | 事 | shì |
| 回 | 回 | 回 | 回 | 回 | 回 | huí |
| 跟 | 跟 | 跟 | 跟 | 跟 | 跟 | gēn |
| 起 | 起 | 起 | 起 | 起 | 起 | qǐ |
| 电 | 电 | 电 | 电 | 电 | 电 | diàn |
| 影 | 影 | 影 | 影 | 影 | 影 | yǐng |
| 咖 | 咖 | 咖 | 咖 | 咖 | 咖 | kā |
| 啡 | 啡 | 啡 | 啡 | 啡 | 啡 | fēi |
| 半 | 半 | 半 | 半 | 半 | 半 | bàn |

| 等 | 等 | 等 | 等 | 等 | 等 | děng |
|---|---|---|---|---|---|---|
| 走 | 走 | 走 | 走 | 走 | 走 | zǒu |

2. 按正确笔顺临写下列汉字：

Copy the following characters in the correct stroke-order:

| 点 | | | | | | | |
|---|---|---|---|---|---|---|---|
| 食 | | | | | | | |
| 堂 | | | | | | | |
| 差 | | | | | | | |
| 分 | | | | | | | |
| 刻 | | | | | | | |
| 课 | | | | | | | |
| 以 | | | | | | | |
| 后 | | | | | | | |

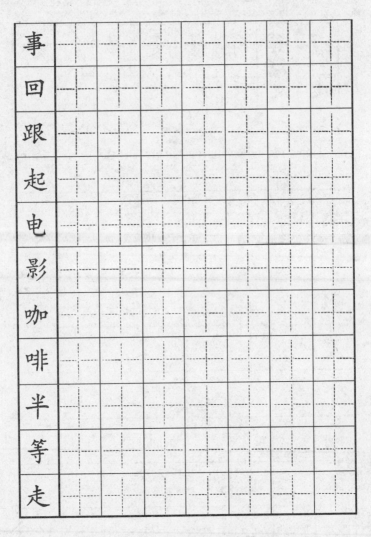

事
回
跟
起
电
影
咖
啡
半
等
走

3. 给下列汉字注音，把相同的偏旁写在（　）中：
Write each of the following characters in phonetic
transcription and put in the brackets the component

108

that the characters in each group have in common:

走_____ 起_____（　　）

口_____ 喝_____ 咖_____

啡_____ 吗_____（　　）

堂_____ 地_____ 在_____

坐_____（　　）

等_____ 笔_____（　　）

课_____ 语_____ 词_____

说_____（　　）

4. 将下列同音字组成词语写在（　　）中：
Make up words or phrases with each of the homonymous characters in each pair and put what you have
made in the brackets:

kè { 客（　　）
　　 课（　　）

shí { 十（　　）
　　 食（　　）

shì { 事（　　）
　　 室（　　）

diǎn { 典（　　）
　　　点（　　）

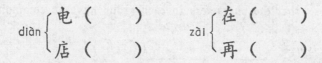

diàn {电 ( ) 店 ( )    zài {在 ( ) 再 ( )

5. 给下列各组形近字注音并组成词语:
Write in phonetic transcription the characters similar in shape and structure in each pair, then make up words or phrases with each and put what you have made in the brackets:

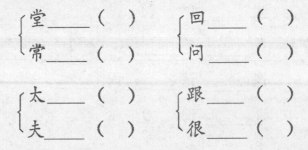

堂＿＿＿ ( )     回＿＿＿ ( )
常＿＿＿ ( )     问＿＿＿ ( )

太＿＿＿ ( )     跟＿＿＿ ( )
夫＿＿＿ ( )     很＿＿＿ ( )

6. 想一想,在下面空格中写一个什么字,就组成四个汉字:
Try to fill in the square at the centre with a component that forms a character with any of the four component enclosed in the squares at the top, bottom and sides:

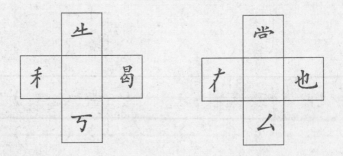

# 第十八课 Lesson 18

一、汉字分析

Analysis of Characters

1. 怎样写合体字

How to write compound characters

写合体字要注意字的间架结构，注意各结构单位的笔画、笔顺。利用汉字课本中的田字格，掌握好合体字结构单位的比例。例如：

In writing a compound character, care must first of all be taken to make the skeleton well-balanced. Care must also be taken to follow the proper order of the strokes and the components so that the component parts stand in correct position to each other. The cross-squares provided in this book will be very useful in helping learners write a good hand.E.g.

| 男 | （上下相等　The top component and the bottom component of equal size) |
| 说 | （左边小右边大　The left-hand component smaller than the right-hand one) |
| 刻 | （左边大右边小　The left-hand component bigger than the right-hand one) |
| 家 | （上面小下面大　The top component smaller than the bottom one) |

111

想 （上面大下面小 The top component bigger than the bottom one)

2. 汉字偏旁
Character component

饭 ⎰ 饣 （食字旁 shízìpáng the component "饣"）
⎱ 反

食字旁的汉字大都与食物名称和饮食动作有关。
The meaning of characters containing the component "饣" usually has something to do with some kind of food or the act of eating.

二、汉字练习
Character Exercises

1. 按正确笔顺描写下列汉字：
Trace the following characters in the correct stroke-order:

| 天 | 天 | 天 | 天 | 天 | 天 | tiān |
| 每 | 每 | 每 | 每 | 每 | 每 | měi |
| 床 | 床 | 床 | 床 | 床 | 床 | chuáng |
| 午 | 午 | 午 | 午 | 午 | 午 | wǔ |

112

| | | | | | | |
|---|---|---|---|---|---|---|
| 饭 | 饭 | 饭 | 饭 | 饭 | 饭 | fàn |
| 休 | 休 | 休 | 休 | 休 | 休 | xiū |
| 息 | 息 | 息 | 息 | 息 | 息 | xī |
| 时 | 时 | 时 | 时 | 时 | 时 | shí |
| 候 | 候 | 候 | 候 | 候 | 候 | hòu |
| 题 | 题 | 题 | 题 | 题 | 题 | tí |
| 睡 | 睡 | 睡 | 睡 | 睡 | 睡 | shuì |
| 觉 | 觉 | 觉 | 觉 | 觉 | 觉 | jiào |
| 吃 | 吃 | 吃 | 吃 | 吃 | 吃 | chī |

2. 按正确笔顺临写下列汉字:

Copy the following characters in the correct stroke-order

| | | | | | | | | |
|---|---|---|---|---|---|---|---|---|
| 天 | | | | | | | | |
| 每 | | | | | | | | |

| 床 | | | | | | | | |
| 午 | | | | | | | | |
| 饭 | | | | | | | | |
| 休 | | | | | | | | |
| 息 | | | | | | | | |
| 时 | | | | | | | | |
| 候 | | | | | | | | |
| 吃 | | | | | | | | |
| 题 | | | | | | | | |
| 睡 | | | | | | | | |
| 觉 | | | | | | | | |

3．分析下列汉字结构，把它填入结构示意图后的方格中：
Analyze the arrangement of the component parts of
each of the following characters and write the

114

characters in the squares in the mannner shown in the diagrams given on the left:

休息　睡觉　吃饭　喝茶　时候

4．根据拼音写出下列偏旁的汉字：

Write out the characters that the phonetic transcriptions in each group stand for, containing the component given on the left:

⺮： bǐ＿＿＿＿＿＿　　　děng＿＿＿＿＿＿

广： diàn＿＿＿＿＿＿　　chuáng＿＿＿＿＿＿

心： xiǎng＿＿＿＿＿　　zhǐ＿＿＿＿＿＿　　xī＿＿＿＿＿＿

攵： jiāo＿＿＿＿＿＿　　gǎn＿＿＿＿＿＿

禾 ： qún＿＿＿＿＿＿ chèn＿＿＿＿＿＿ shān＿＿＿＿＿＿

走 ： zǒu＿＿＿＿＿＿ qǐ＿＿＿＿＿＿

饣 ： fàn＿＿＿＿＿＿ guǎn＿＿＿＿＿＿

口 ： chī＿＿＿＿＿＿ hē＿＿＿＿＿＿

目 ： shuì＿＿＿＿＿＿ kàn＿＿＿＿＿＿

5. 给下列各组形近字注音并组成词语：
Write in phonetic transcription the characters similar in shape and structure in each pair, then make up words or phrases with each and put what you have made in the brackets:

夫＿＿＿＿＿（　　）　　觉＿＿＿＿＿（　　）

天＿＿＿＿＿（　　）　　览＿＿＿＿＿（　　）

这＿＿＿＿＿（　　）　　学＿＿＿＿＿（　　）

还＿＿＿＿＿（　　）　　字＿＿＿＿＿（　　）

6. 找出下面的错字并改正，把正确的写在（　　）中：
Pick out the wrongly written characters in the following words and phrases, then write the correct forms in the brackets:

写汉字（　　）　　有时侯（　　）

告诉　（　　）　　食常（　　　）

三点三分（　　）　　回家（　　　）

新书　（　　）　　朋友（　　　）

穿衬衫（　　　）

7. 猜字谜：
   Guess the riddle about a Chinese character:

   "人"有他是大，

   "天"没他是大。

   这是什么字，

   你也认识他。（猜一个汉字，谜底见下课。
   The solution to the riddle is a
   Chinese character, given in Les-
   son 19.)

# 第十九课 Lesson 19

一、汉字分析

Analysis of characters

### 1. 合体字书写顺序

The order of component parts for writing compound characters

内外结构（一）

one component part enclosed in another (1)

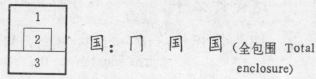

国：冂 囯 国（全包围 Total enclosure）

### 2. 汉字偏旁

Character component

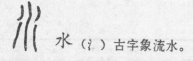

酒 { 氵 { 酉
wine

（三点水 sāndiǎnshuǐ the component"氵"）

川 水（氵）古字象流水。

水（氵）旁的字大都是和液体有关，如酒。

The component "氵" is a variant of the character "水"

118

derived from the ideogram "⺌⺌" symbolizing flowing water. Therefore, characters containing "氵" usually have something to to with liquid, e.g. "酒".

二、汉字练习

Character Exercises

1. 按正确笔顺描写下列汉字：

Trace the following characters in the correct stroke-order:

| | | | | | | |
|---|---|---|---|---|---|---|
| 要 | 要 | 要 | 要 | 要 | 要 | yào |
| 服 | 服 | 服 | 服 | 服 | 服 | fú |
| 务 | 务 | 务 | 务 | 务 | 务 | wù |
| 员 | 员 | 员 | 员 | 员 | 员 | yuán |
| 喜 | 喜 | 喜 | 喜 | 喜 | 喜 | xǐ |
| 花 | 花 | 花 | 花 | 花 | 花 | huā |
| 红 | 红 | 红 | 红 | 红 | 红 | hóng |
| 桔 | 桔 | 桔 | 桔 | 桔 | 桔 | jú |

| | | | | | | |
|---|---|---|---|---|---|---|
| 水 | 水 | 水 | 水 | 水 | 水 | shuǐ |
| 杯 | 杯 | 杯 | 杯 | 杯 | 杯 | bēi |
| 瓶 | 瓶 | 瓶 | 瓶 | 瓶 | 瓶 | píng |
| 啤 | 啤 | 啤 | 啤 | 啤 | 啤 | pí |
| 酒 | 酒 | 酒 | 酒 | 酒 | 酒 | jiǔ |
| 听 | 听 | 听 | 听 | 听 | 听 | tīng |
| 民 | 民 | 民 | 民 | 民 | 民 | mín |
| 歌 | 歌 | 歌 | 歌 | 歌 | 歌 | gē |
| 古 | 古 | 古 | 古 | 古 | 古 | gǔ |
| 音 | 音 | 音 | 音 | 音 | 音 | yīn |
| 乐 | 乐 | 乐 | 乐 | 乐 | 乐 | yuè |
| 代 | 代 | 代 | 代 | 代 | 代 | dài |
| 唱 | 唱 | 唱 | 唱 | 唱 | 唱 | chàng |

| | | | | | | |
|---|---|---|---|---|---|---|
| 让 | 让 | 让 | 让 | 让 | 让 | ràng |
| 别 | 别 | 别 | 别 | 别 | 别 | bié |

2. 按正确笔顺临写下列汉字:

Copy the following characters in the correct stroke-order:

| | | | | | | | | |
|---|---|---|---|---|---|---|---|---|
| 要 | | | | | | | | |
| 服 | | | | | | | | |
| 务 | | | | | | | | |
| 员 | | | | | | | | |
| 喜 | | | | | | | | |
| 花 | | | | | | | | |
| 红 | | | | | | | | |
| 桔 | | | | | | | | |
| 水 | | | | | | | | |

杯

瓶

啤

酒

听

民

歌

古

音

乐

代

唱

| 让 | | | | | | | |
|---|---|---|---|---|---|---|---|
| 别 | | | | | | | |

3. 给下列各组汉字注音，把相同的偏旁写在（　　）中：
Write each of the following characters in phonetic transcription and put in the brackets the component that the characters in each group have in common:

酒＿＿＿＿汉＿＿＿＿没＿＿＿＿（　）

花＿＿＿＿茶＿＿＿＿（　）

喝＿＿＿＿吃＿＿＿＿唱＿＿＿＿（　）

刻＿＿＿＿别＿＿＿＿（　）

4. 给下列各组形近字注音并组成词语：
Write in phonetic transcription the character similar in shape and structure in each pair, then make up words or phrases with each and put what you have made in the brackets:

唱＿＿＿（　）　　叫＿＿＿（　）

喝＿＿＿（　）　　听＿＿＿（　）

要＿＿＿（　）　　小＿＿＿（　）

票＿＿＿（　）　　少＿＿＿（　）

5. 根据拼音写汉字：

Put the phonetic transcriptions in the following phrases into Chinese characters:

喝 hóng chá _____ 喝 píjiǔ _____

要 kāfēi _____ 要 júzishuǐ _____

hái _____ 有一本书 huán _____ 你一本书

6. 猜字谜：

Guess the riddle about a Chinese character:

一字有两口，大口吃小口。

(猜一汉字，谜底见下课。

The solution to the riddle is a Chinese character, given in Lesson 20.)

(上课谜底是"一"字。

The solution to the riddle in Lesson 18 is the character "一".)

# 第二十课 Lesson 20

## 一、汉字分析
### Analysis of Characters

#### 汉字偏旁
#### Character components

期 { 其
　　月 (月字旁 yuèzìpáng the component "月")

月 古字象不圆的月亮。
The component "月" originated from the
ideogram "Ɒ" symbolizing the new moon.

月字旁的字与时间有关，如"期"。
The meaning of characters containing "月" usually has
something to do with time, e.g. "期".

星 { 日 (日字头 (rìzìtóu the top component "日")
　　生

晚 { 日 (日字旁 rìzìpáng the component "日")
　　免

日　古字象太阳。

The component "日" developed from the ideogram "⊖" or "☉" symbolizing the sun.

日旁的字大都与季节和时间有关。如"星（期）"、"晚"、"时"等。

The meaning of characters containing "日" has something to do with time or the seasons of the year in most cases, e.g. "星（期）", "晚" and "时" etc.

二、汉字练习

Character Exercises

1. 按正确的笔顺描写下列汉字：

Trace the following characters in the correct stroke-order:

| | | | | | | |
|---|---|---|---|---|---|---|
| 月 | 月 | 月 | 月 | 月 | 月 | yuè |
| 日 | 日 | 日 | 日 | 日 | 日 | rì |
| 辅 | 辅 | 辅 | 辅 | 辅 | 辅 | fǔ |
| 导 | 导 | 导 | 导 | 导 | 导 | dǎo |
| 空 | 空 | 空 | 空 | 空 | 空 | kòng |
| 今 | 今 | 今 | 今 | 今 | 今 | jīn |

| | | | | | | |
|---|---|---|---|---|---|---|
| 年 | 年 | 年 | 年 | 年 | 年 | nián |
| 岁 | 岁 | 岁 | 岁 | 岁 | 岁 | suì |
| 祝 | 祝 | 祝 | 祝 | 祝 | 祝 | zhù |
| 贺 | 贺 | 贺 | 贺 | 贺 | 贺 | hè |
| 舞 | 舞 | 舞 | 舞 | 舞 | 舞 | wǔ |
| 会 | 会 | 会 | 会 | 会 | 会 | huì |
| 参 | 参 | 参 | 参 | 参 | 参 | cān |
| 加 | 加 | 加 | 加 | 加 | 加 | jiā |
| 班 | 班 | 班 | 班 | 班 | 班 | bān |
| 定 | 定 | 定 | 定 | 定 | 定 | dìng |
| 意 | 意 | 意 | 意 | 意 | 意 | yì |
| 思 | 思 | 思 | 思 | 思 | 思 | sī |
| 星 | 星 | 星 | 星 | 星 | 星 | xīng |

| | | | | | | |
|---|---|---|---|---|---|---|
| 期 | 期 | 期 | 期 | 期 | 期 | qī |
| 知 | 知 | 知 | 知 | 知 | 知 | zhī |
| 道 | 道 | 道 | 道 | 道 | 道 | dào |
| 址 | 址 | 址 | 址 | 址 | 址 | zhǐ |

2. 按正确的笔顺临写下列汉字:
Copy the following characters in the correct stroke-order:

| | | | | | | | |
|---|---|---|---|---|---|---|---|
| 月 | | | | | | | |
| 日 | | | | | | | |
| 辅 | | | | | | | |
| 导 | | | | | | | |
| 空 | | | | | | | |
| 今 | | | | | | | |
| 年 | | | | | | | |

128

| 岁 | | | | | | | |
| 祝 | | | | | | | |
| 贺 | | | | | | | |
| 舞 | | | | | | | |
| 会 | | | | | | | |
| 参 | | | | | | | |
| 加 | | | | | | | |
| 班 | | | | | | | |
| 定 | | | | | | | |
| 意 | | | | | | | |
| 思 | | | | | | | |
| 星 | | | | | | | |

| 期 | | | | | | | | |
|---|---|---|---|---|---|---|---|---|
| 知 | | | | | | | | |
| 道 | | | | | | | | |
| 址 | | | | | | | | |

3. 给下列各汉字注音，把相同的偏旁写在（  ）中：
Write each of the following characters in phonetic transcription and put in the brackets the component that the characters in each group have in common:

日_____ 星_____ 晚_____ 时_____

是_____ （    ）

月_____ 期_____ （    ）

人_____ 介_____ 会_____ 今_____

个_____ 舍_____ （    ）

意_____ 思_____ 想_____ 志_____

息_____ （    ）

4. 将下列同音字组成词语写在（  ）中：
Make up words or phrases with each of the homony-

mous characters in each pair and put what you have
made in the brackets:

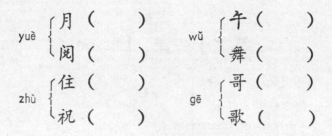

5. 用汉字写出今天是几月几号星期几？

Write in Chinese characters what day and date it is
todoy.

（上一课谜底是"回"字。

The solution to the riddle in lesson 18 is the character "回"。）

# 第二十一课　Lesson 21

一、汉字分析

Analysis of Characters

1. 合体字的书写顺序

The order of component parts for writing compound characters

内外结构（二）

One component part enclosed in the other (2).

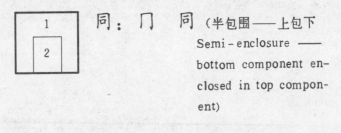

同：冂　同 （半包围——上包下
Semi‑enclosure ——
bottom component en‑
closed in top compon‑
ent)

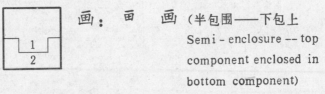

画：画　画 （半包围——下包上
Semi‑enclosure -- top
component enclosed in
bottom component)

2. 汉字偏旁

Character components

132

跳 ⎰ 𧾷 （足字旁 zúzìpáng the component "足"）
   ⎱ 兆

足 （𧾷） 古字象脚。

足字旁的字大都是与脚有关，如"跳"、"跟"。

The component "𧾷" is a variant of the character "足" developed from the above ancient ideogram symbolizing a foot. so characters containing "𧾷" usually have a connotation pertaining to feet or actions performed by feet.

cming

祝 ⎰ 礻 （示字旁 shìzìpáng the component "礻"）
   ⎱ 兄

示字旁的字大都与祭祀、祝福有关，如"祝贺"的"祝"。

The meaning of characters containing the component "礻" usually has something to do with blessing or sacrificial rites, e.g "祝" in the word "祝贺".

二、汉字练习
Character Exercises

1. 按正确的笔顺描写下列汉字:
Trace the following characters in the correct stroke-order:

| | | | | | | |
|---|---|---|---|---|---|---|
| 束 | 束 | 束 | 束 | 束 | 束 | shù |
| 送 | 送 | 送 | 送 | 送 | 送 | sòng |
| 真 | 真 | 真 | 真 | 真 | 真 | zhēn |
| 非 | 非 | 非 | 非 | 非 | 非 | fēi |
| 感 | 感 | 感 | 感 | 感 | 感 | gǎn |
| 高 | 高 | 高 | 高 | 高 | 高 | gāo |
| 兴 | 兴 | 兴 | 兴 | 兴 | 兴 | xìng |
| 轻 | 轻 | 轻 | 轻 | 轻 | 轻 | qīng |
| 跳 | 跳 | 跳 | 跳 | 跳 | 跳 | tiào |
| 吧 | 吧 | 吧 | 吧 | 吧 | 吧 | ba |
| 姑 | 姑 | 姑 | 姑 | 姑 | 姑 | gū |

| | | | | | | |
|---|---|---|---|---|---|---|
| 娘 | 娘 | 娘 | 娘 | 娘 | 娘 | niáng |
| 漂 | 漂 | 漂 | 漂 | 漂 | 漂 | piào |
| 亮 | 亮 | 亮 | 亮 | 亮 | 亮 | liàng |
| 更 | 更 | 更 | 更 | 更 | 更 | gèng |
| 象 | 象 | 象 | 象 | 象 | 象 | xiàng |
| 开 | 开 | 开 | 开 | 开 | 开 | kāi |
| 门 | 门 | 门 | 门 | 门 | 门 | mén |

2. 按正确的笔顺临写下列汉字：

Copy the following characters in the correct stroke-order:

| | | | | | | | | |
|---|---|---|---|---|---|---|---|---|
| 束 | | | | | | | | |
| 送 | | | | | | | | |
| 真 | | | | | | | | |
| 非 | | | | | | | | |

感

高

兴

轻

跳

吧

姑

娘

漂

亮

更

象

| 开 | | | | | | | |
|---|---|---|---|---|---|---|---|
| 门 | | | | | | | |

**3.** 给下列汉字注音，把相同的偏旁写在（ ）中：

Write each of the following characters in phonetic transcription and put in the brackets the component that the characters in each group have in common:

跳＿＿＿跟＿＿＿（ ）

漂＿＿＿酒＿＿＿汉＿＿＿没＿＿＿

法＿＿＿（ ）

**4.** 抄写本课书中有下列偏旁的汉字：

Write out the characters occuring in this lesson, containing each of the components given at the head:

女：＿＿＿ ＿＿＿ ＿＿＿ ＿＿＿

讠：＿＿＿ ＿＿＿ ＿＿＿ ＿＿＿

辶：＿＿＿ ＿＿＿ ＿＿＿ ＿＿＿

**5.** 将下列各组同音字组成词语写在（ ）中：

make up words or phrases with each of the homonymous characters in each pair and put what you have made in the brackets:

$$
gǎn \begin{cases} 感 (\quad) \\ 敢 (\quad) \end{cases} \qquad piào \begin{cases} 票 (\quad) \\ 漂 (\quad) \end{cases}
$$

$$
xìng \begin{cases} 姓 (\quad) \\ 兴 (\quad) \end{cases} \qquad zuò \begin{cases} 坐 (\quad) \\ 作 (\quad) \end{cases}
$$

6. 将下列拼音写成汉字:
   Put the following phrases in phonetic transcription
   into Chinese characters:

   zhēn niánqīng _____

   hěn hǎokàn _____

   gèng piàoliang _____

   fēicháng gāoxìng _____

# 第二十二课　Lesson 22

一、汉字分析

Analysis of Characters

1. 合体字的书写顺序

The order of component parts for writing compound
characters

内外结构（三）

One component part enclosed in the other (3)。

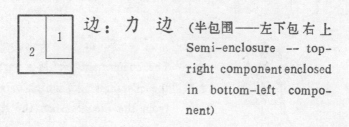

边：力　边 （半包围——左下包右上
Semi-enclosure -- top-
right component enclosed
in bottom-left compo-
nent)

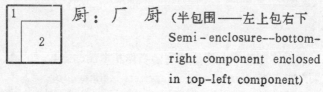

厨：厂　厨 （半包围——左上包右下
Semi-enclosure--bottom-
right component enclosed
in top-left component)

2. 汉字偏旁

Character components

139

间 { 门 （门字框 ménzìkuàng the component "门"）

门 日

門 门　古字象门。

门字框的字大都与门有关。

The component "门" is the simplified form of the character "門" which came from the ideogram "門" symbolizing a door or gate. That is why characters containing "门" usually have something to do with doors.

椅 { 木 （木字旁 mùzìpáng the component "木"）

奇

木 (木)　古字象树形。

The component "木" is a variant of the character "木" which originated from the ideogram on the left symbolizing a tree.

木字旁的字大都是植物的名称和木制的器具，如"桌"、"椅"。

The meaning of characters containing "木" usually has something to do with plants or wooden furniture, e.g. "桌"、"椅".

140

二、汉字练习

Character Exercises

1. 按正确的笔顺描写下列汉字：

Trace the following characters in the correct stroke-order:

| | | | | | | |
|---|---|---|---|---|---|---|
| 边 | 边 | 边 | 边 | 边 | 边 | biān |
| 小 | 小 | 小 | 小 | 小 | 小 | xiǎo |
| 园 | 园 | 园 | 园 | 园 | 园 | yuán |
| 房 | 房 | 房 | 房 | 房 | 房 | fáng |
| 厅 | 厅 | 厅 | 厅 | 厅 | 厅 | tīng |
| 里 | 里 | 里 | 里 | 里 | 里 | lǐ |
| 旁 | 旁 | 旁 | 旁 | 旁 | 旁 | páng |
| 椅 | 椅 | 椅 | 椅 | 椅 | 椅 | yǐ |
| 桌 | 桌 | 桌 | 桌 | 桌 | 桌 | zhuō |
| 总 | 总 | 总 | 总 | 总 | 总 | zǒng |
| 整 | 整 | 整 | 整 | 整 | 整 | zhěng |

| | | | | | |
|---|---|---|---|---|---|
| 理 | 理 | 理 | 理 | 理 | 理 | lǐ |
| 厨 | 厨 | 厨 | 厨 | 厨 | 厨 | chú |
| 面 | 面 | 面 | 面 | 面 | 面 | miàn |
| 帮 | 帮 | 帮 | 帮 | 帮 | 帮 | bāng |
| 助 | 助 | 助 | 助 | 助 | 助 | zhù |
| 餐 | 餐 | 餐 | 餐 | 餐 | 餐 | cān |
| 左 | 左 | 左 | 左 | 左 | 左 | zuǒ |
| 间 | 间 | 间 | 间 | 间 | 间 | jiān |
| 卧 | 卧 | 卧 | 卧 | 卧 | 卧 | wò |
| 洗 | 洗 | 洗 | 洗 | 洗 | 洗 | xǐ |
| 澡 | 澡 | 澡 | 澡 | 澡 | 澡 | zǎo |
| 怎 | 怎 | 怎 | 怎 | 怎 | 怎 | zěn |
| 样 | 样 | 样 | 样 | 样 | 样 | yàng |

**2.** 按正确的笔顺临写下列汉字：

Copy the following characters in the correct stroke-order:

| 边 | | | | | | | |
|---|---|---|---|---|---|---|---|
| 小 | | | | | | | |
| 园 | | | | | | | |
| 房 | | | | | | | |
| 厅 | | | | | | | |
| 里 | | | | | | | |
| 旁 | | | | | | | |
| 椅 | | | | | | | |
| 桌 | | | | | | | |
| 总 | | | | | | | |
| 整 | | | | | | | |

| 理 |  |  |  |  |  |  |  |  |  |
|---|---|---|---|---|---|---|---|---|---|
| 厨 |  |  |  |  |  |  |  |  |  |
| 面 |  |  |  |  |  |  |  |  |  |
| 帮 |  |  |  |  |  |  |  |  |  |
| 助 |  |  |  |  |  |  |  |  |  |
| 餐 |  |  |  |  |  |  |  |  |  |
| 左 |  |  |  |  |  |  |  |  |  |
| 间 |  |  |  |  |  |  |  |  |  |
| 卧 |  |  |  |  |  |  |  |  |  |
| 洗 |  |  |  |  |  |  |  |  |  |
| 澡 |  |  |  |  |  |  |  |  |  |
| 怎 |  |  |  |  |  |  |  |  |  |

| 样 | | | | | | | | | |
|---|---|---|---|---|---|---|---|---|---|

3. 写出带下列偏旁的汉字：

Write out the characters containing each of the following components given at the head:

木：_____  _____  _____

氵：_____  _____  _____

  _____

厂：_____  _____

门：_____  _____

辶：_____  _____    _____  _____

4. 把下列各组同音字组成词语：

make up words or phrases with each of the homonymous characters in each pair and put what you have made in the brackets:

tīng { 厅（      ）   lǐ { 理（      ）
     { 听（      ）      { 里（      ）

yǐ { 以（      ）   shì { 室（      ）
   { 椅（      ）       { 事（      ）

145

5. 用下列汉字组成词语:

Fill in each blank with a character that form a word
or phrase with the character given:

_____边 _____边 _____边 _____边

_____边 _____边

_____厅 _____厅

_____室 _____室

_____子 _____子 _____子 _____子

_____子

6. 试在"房"字四边的空格中各写一个汉字,组成四个本课
学过的词:

Try to put in each of the four empty boxes a character that forms with "房" in the box at the centre a
word taught in the present lesson:

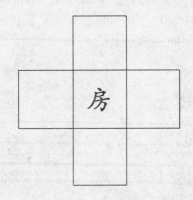

7. 猜字谜:

Guess the riddle about a Chinese character:

左边一个月，右边一个月。

左边和右边，写了两个月。

（猜一汉字，谜底见下课。
The solution to the riddle is a
Chinese character, given in
Lesson 23.）

# 第二十三课  Lesson 23

一、汉字分析
Analysis of Characters
汉字偏旁
Character component

$$接\begin{cases} 扌 \\ 妾 \end{cases}$$ 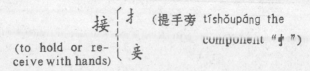（提手旁 tíshǒupáng the component "扌"）

(to hold or receive with hands)

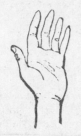 

手（扌）古字象手。
The component "扌" is a variant of the character "手" which came from the ideogram on the left symbolizing a hand.

提手旁的字大都表示动作，如接、打、找等。
The meaning of characters containing "扌" usually has something to do with actions performed by the hands, e.g. "接", "打" and "找" etc.

$$照\begin{cases} 昭 \\ 灬 \end{cases}$$

(illuminate) 灬（四点底 sìdiǎndǐ the bottom component "灬"）

148

"灬"——古字表示火，"照"要用火。

In ancient ideogram the bottom component "灬" symbolized a tongue of flame. The character "照" containing "灬" means "to shine or illuminate".

二、汉字练习

Character Exercises

1. 按正确笔顺描写下列汉字：

Trace the following characters in the correct stroke-order:

| | | | | | | |
|---|---|---|---|---|---|---|
| 正 | 正 | 正 | 正 | 正 | 正 | zhěng |
| 视 | 视 | 视 | 视 | 视 | 视 | shì |
| 接 | 接 | 接 | 接 | 接 | 接 | jiē |
| 话 | 话 | 话 | 话 | 话 | 话 | huà |
| 复 | 复 | 复 | 复 | 复 | 复 | fù |
| 闻 | 闻 | 闻 | 闻 | 闻 | 闻 | wén |
| 表 | 表 | 表 | 表 | 表 | 表 | biǎo |
| 团 | 团 | 团 | 团 | 团 | 团 | tuán |

| | | | | | | |
|---|---|---|---|---|---|---|
| 观 | 观 | 观 | 观 | 观 | 观 | guān |
| 厂 | 厂 | 厂 | 厂 | 厂 | 厂 | chǎng |
| 访 | 访 | 访 | 访 | 访 | 访 | fǎng |
| 照 | 照 | 照 | 照 | 照 | 照 | zhào |
| 片 | 片 | 片 | 片 | 片 | 片 | piàn |
| 打 | 打 | 打 | 打 | 打 | 打 | dǎ |
| 明 | 明 | 明 | 明 | 明 | 明 | míng |
| 城 | 城 | 城 | 城 | 城 | 城 | chéng |
| 玩 | 玩 | 玩 | 玩 | 玩 | 玩 | wán |
| 出 | 出 | 出 | 出 | 出 | 出 | chū |
| 发 | 发 | 发 | 发 | 发 | 发 | fā |

2. 按正确笔顺临写下列汉字：

Copy the following characters in the correct stroke-order:

150

正
视
接
话
复
闻
表
团
观
厂
访
照

| 片 | | | | | | |
|---|---|---|---|---|---|---|
| 打 | | | | | | |
| 明 | | | | | | |
| 城 | | | | | | |
| 玩 | | | | | | |
| 出 | | | | | | |
| 发 | | | | | | |

3. 给下列汉字注音，把相同的偏旁写在（　　）中：
Write each of the following characters in phonetic
transcription and put in the brackets the component
that the characters in each group have in common:

打＿＿＿＿＿接 ＿＿＿＿＿找 ＿＿＿＿＿　（　　　）

照＿＿＿＿＿点 ＿＿＿＿＿　　　　　　　（　　　）

地＿＿＿＿＿城 ＿＿＿＿＿　　　　　　　（　　　）

明＿＿＿＿＿晚 ＿＿＿＿＿时 ＿＿＿＿＿　（　　　）

4. 写出本课书中有下列偏旁的汉字：

Write out the characters occuring in this lesson, containing each of the following components given at the head:

心：＿＿＿　＿＿＿

讠：＿＿＿　＿＿＿　＿＿＿　＿＿＿

亻：＿＿＿　＿＿＿　＿＿＿　＿＿＿　＿＿＿

5. 给下列各组形近字注音并组词：

Write in phonetic transcription the characters similar in shape and structure in each pair, then make up words or phrases with each and put what you have made in the brackets:

祝＿＿＿（　　）　欢＿＿＿（　　）
视＿＿＿（　　）　观＿＿＿（　　）

间＿＿＿（　　）　朋＿＿＿（　　）
闻＿＿＿（　　）　明＿＿＿（　　）

发＿＿＿（　　）　找＿＿＿（　　）
友＿＿＿（　　）　我＿＿＿（　　）

6. 把下列词中的拼音写成汉字：

Write out the characters that the phonetic transcriptions in the following words or phrases stand for:

新 wén _____        电 huà _____

课 wén _____        fǎng _____ 问

xué _____ 习        qǐng _____ 问

fù _____ 习         工 rén _____

参 jiā _____         工 chǎng _____

参 guān _____        工 zuò

电 shì _____         péng _____ 友

电 yǐng _____        友 hǎo _____

（上课谜底：朋。

The solution to the riddle in Lesson 22 is the character "朋".)

# 第二十四课　Lesson 24

一、汉字分析

Analysis of Characters

1. 怎样写合体字

How to write compound characters

| | |
|---|---|
| 朋 | （左右相等　The left-hand and right-hand componems of equal size) |
| 谢 | （左中右相等　The left-hand , middle and right-hand components of equal size) |
| 锻 | （左中右不等　The left-hand, middle and right-hand components not of equal size) |
| 意 | （上中下相等　The top, middle and bottom components of equal size) |

2. 汉字偏旁：

Character components

炼 ｛ 火 （火字旁 huǒzìpáng the component "火")
东

火（火）

古字象火的形状。

The component "火" is a variant of the character "火" which originated from the ideogram on the left symbolizing a tongue of flame.

火字旁的汉字跟火有关。

So the meaning of characters containing "火" usually has something to do with fire or things connected with fire.

练 ⎰ 纟（绞丝旁 jiǎosīpáng the component "纟"）
　　⎱ 东

帛　糸　纟　古字象一束丝。用绞丝旁的汉字原与丝有关。

The component "纟" originated from the above ideogram symbolizing a strand of silk. That is why the meaning of characters containing "纟" originally had something to do with silk or some kind of resemblance to silk.

二、汉字练习

Character Exercises

1. 按正确的笔顺描写下列汉字：

Trace the following characters in the correct stroke-order:

| | | | | | | |
|---|---|---|---|---|---|---|
| 心 | 心 | 心 | 心 | 心 | 心 | xīn |
| 农 | 农 | 农 | 农 | 农 | 农 | nóng |
| 村 | 村 | 村 | 村 | 村 | 村 | cūn |
| 锻 | 锻 | 锻 | 锻 | 锻 | 锻 | duàn |
| 炼 | 炼 | 炼 | 炼 | 炼 | 炼 | liàn |
| 答 | 答 | 答 | 答 | 答 | 答 | dá |
| 些 | 些 | 些 | 些 | 些 | 些 | xiē |
| 难 | 难 | 难 | 难 | 难 | 难 | nán |
| 念 | 念 | 念 | 念 | 念 | 念 | niàn |
| 练 | 练 | 练 | 练 | 练 | 练 | liàn |
| 懂 | 懂 | 懂 | 懂 | 懂 | 懂 | dǒng |

2. 按正确的笔顺临写下列汉字：

Copy the following characters in the correct stroke-order:

| 心 | | | | | | | |
|---|---|---|---|---|---|---|---|
| 农 | | | | | | | |
| 村 | | | | | | | |
| 锻 | | | | | | | |
| 炼 | | | | | | | |
| 答 | | | | | | | |
| 些 | | | | | | | |
| 难 | | | | | | | |
| 念 | | | | | | | |
| 练 | | | | | | | |
| 懂 | | | | | | | |

**3.** 分析下列汉字的结构特点，把它写在结构示意图后的方格中：

Analyze the arrangement of the component parts of each of the following characters in the squares in the manner shown in the diagrams given on the left:

请问　锻炼　欢迎　地图　画报　意思
男朋友　观看　桌椅　语法　时刻　别

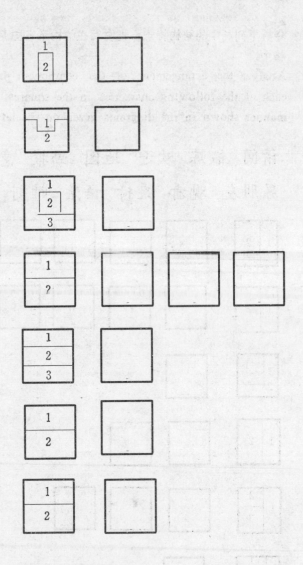

4. 根据拼音写出下列偏旁的汉字：

Put the phonetic transcriptions in each group into

Chinese characters containing the component given on the left:

氵 ： jiǔ _____ xǐ _____ zǎo _____ hàn _____

　　méi _____ fǎ _____ piào _____

月 ： yuè _____ qī _____

日 ： rì _____ wǎn _____ shí _____ míng _____

　　xīng _____ shì _____

足 ： gēn _____ tiào _____

衤 ： zhù _____ shì _____

扌 ： dǎ _____ jiē _____ zhǎo _____

灬 ： zhào _____ diǎn _____

门 ： mén _____ jiān _____ wèn _____

　　wén _____

木 ： yǐ _____ jú _____ zhuō _____ chuáng _____

　　cūn _____

火 ： liàn _____ yān _____

纟 ： liàn _____ shào _____ lǜ _____

　　hóng _____ gěi _____

5. 将下列各组同音字组成词语写在（　　）中：

Make up words or phrases with each of the homonymous characters in each pair and put what you have made in the brackets:

xīn { 新 （　　　）  
　　　心 （　　　）

liàn { 炼 （　　　）  
　　　练 （　　　）

hòu { 后 （　　　）  
　　　候 （　　　）

sù { 诉 （　　　）  
　　　宿 （　　　）

6. 找出下面的错字并改正，把正确的写在（　　）中：

Pick out the wrongly written characters in the following words and phrases, then write the correct forms in the brackets:

听音乐 （　　　）　　　真好看 （　　　）

民歌 　（　　　）　　　跳舞 　（　　　）

同学 　（　　　）　　　服务员 （　　　）

姑娘 　（　　　）　　　电视 　（　　　）

喝茶 　（　　　）

7. 猜字谜：Guess the riddle about a Chinese character:

一人前边走，一人后边走。

他们两个人，总是一起走。

（猜一汉字，谜底见下课。
The solution to the riddle is a
Chinese character given in Le-
sson 25.）

# 第二十五课 Lesson 25

一、汉字分析
## Analysis of Characters

### 1. 形声字
#### Pictophonetic characters

用现成的两个符号，一个表示意义，叫形旁，一个表示声音或近似的声音，叫声旁，合起来表示一个新的意思的字叫形声字。如"妈"字，"女"是形旁，表示这个字所属事物的类别，"马"是声旁，表示这个字的读音。

下面分别介绍形声字的形旁和声旁结合的六种基本类型：

Chinese characters which are made up of two components, a signific component and a phonetic component, are known as pictophonetic characters. The signific component indicates the meaning while the phonetic component indicates the sound. The character "妈", for example, is formed of the signific component "女" indicating the class of what the character refers to, and the phonetic component "马" indicating the sound.

There are six basic ways of combining a signific component and a phonetic component to make a new word. They will be dealt with separately in this lesson and the Lessons that follow.

左形右声：

The signific component on the left, the phonetic component on the left, as in

泳 吗 腿 饭

## 2. 汉字偏旁
Character Components:

腿 ⎰ 月 （肉月旁 ròuyuèpáng the component "月"）
leg ⎱ 退

月 古字象肉块。

"月" was derived from the ideogram on the left symbolizing a piece of flesh.

肉月旁的字大都与人体器官和肉类有关。

Characters containing the component "月" generally have something to do with organs of the human body or flesh of one kind or another.

矿 ⎰ 石 （石字旁 shízìpáng, the component "石"）
⎱ 广

石字旁的字大都与石头有关，如"矿"字。

Characters containing the component "石" usually have a connotation pertaining to stone or rock, e.g. "矿".

Character Exercises

1. 按正确笔顺描写下列汉字：

Trace the following characters in the correct stroke-order:

| | | | | | | |
|---|---|---|---|---|---|---|
| 得 | 得 | 得 | 得 | 得 | 得 | de |
| 停 | 停 | 停 | 停 | 停 | 停 | tíng |
| 游 | 游 | 游 | 游 | 游 | 游 | yóu |
| 泳 | 泳 | 泳 | 泳 | 泳 | 泳 | yǒng |
| 前 | 前 | 前 | 前 | 前 | 前 | qián |
| 河 | 河 | 河 | 河 | 河 | 河 | hé |
| 准 | 准 | 准 | 准 | 准 | 准 | zhǔn |
| 备 | 备 | 备 | 备 | 备 | 备 | bèi |
| 钓 | 钓 | 钓 | 钓 | 钓 | 钓 | diào |
| 鱼 | 鱼 | 鱼 | 鱼 | 鱼 | 鱼 | yú |
| 汤 | 汤 | 汤 | 汤 | 汤 | 汤 | tāng |

| | | | | | | |
|---|---|---|---|---|---|---|
| 位 | 位 | 位 | 位 | 位 | 位 | wèi |
| 快 | 快 | 快 | 快 | 快 | 快 | kuài |
| 慢 | 慢 | 慢 | 慢 | 慢 | 慢 | màn |
| 错 | 错 | 错 | 错 | 错 | 错 | cuò |
| 包 | 包 | 包 | 包 | 包 | 包 | bāo |
| 腿 | 腿 | 腿 | 腿 | 腿 | 腿 | tuǐ |
| 奶 | 奶 | 奶 | 奶 | 奶 | 奶 | nǎi |
| 酪 | 酪 | 酪 | 酪 | 酪 | 酪 | lào |
| 矿 | 矿 | 矿 | 矿 | 矿 | 矿 | kuàng |
| 泉 | 泉 | 泉 | 泉 | 泉 | 泉 | quán |
| 火 | 火 | 火 | 火 | 火 | 火 | huǒ |

2. 按正确笔顺临写下列汉字：

Copy the following characters in the correct stroke-order:

| 得 | | | | | | | |
|---|---|---|---|---|---|---|---|
| 停 | | | | | | | |
| 游 | | | | | | | |
| 泳 | | | | | | | |
| 前 | | | | | | | |
| 河 | | | | | | | |
| 准 | | | | | | | |
| 备 | | | | | | | |
| 钓 | | | | | | | |
| 鱼 | | | | | | | |
| 汤 | | | | | | | |
| 位 | | | | | | | |

| 快 | | | | | | | |
| 慢 | | | | | | | |
| 错 | | | | | | | |
| 包 | | | | | | | |
| 腿 | | | | | | | |
| 奶 | | | | | | | |
| 酪 | | | | | | | |
| 矿 | | | | | | | |
| 泉 | | | | | | | |
| 火 | | | | | | | |

3. 抄写本课课文中有下列偏旁的汉字：

Write out the characters occuring in this lesson, containing each of the following components given at
the head:

氵： ＿＿ ＿＿

亻： ＿＿ ＿＿ ＿＿ ＿＿

口： ＿＿ ＿＿ ＿＿ ＿＿

＿＿

4. 给下列汉字注音，把相同的部分写在（　　）中：
Write each of the following characters in phonetic transcription and put in the brackets the component that the characters have in common:

那＿＿＿＿ 哪＿＿＿＿ （　　　）

古＿＿＿＿ 姑＿＿＿＿ （　　　）

非＿＿＿＿ 啡＿＿＿＿ （　　　）

人＿＿＿＿ 认＿＿＿＿ （　　　）

（上课谜底是"从"字。

The solution to the riddle in

lesson 24 is the character "从".）

# 第二十六课　Lesson 26

一、汉字分析

Analysis of Characters

1. 形声字

Pictophonetic characters

右形左声：

The signific component on the right, the phonetic component on the left, as in

翻　期　歌　瓶

2. 汉字偏旁

Character components

加 { 力 （力字旁 lìzìpáng the component "力"）
    口

力　力　古字象筋肉用力的形状。

The component "力" developed from the above ideogram symbolizing a muscle being strained to produce force.

力字旁的字大都与力气有关。

Therefore, the meaning of characters containing "力" usually connotes force or physical strength.

究 { 穴（穴字头 xuézìtóu the component "穴"）
    九

穴　古字表示土屋子或洞穴。

The component "穴" came from the ideogram on the left symbolizing a mud hut or a cave.

二、汉字练习

Character Exercises

1. 按正确笔顺描写下列汉字：

Trace the following characters in the correct stroke-order:

| | | | | | | |
|---|---|---|---|---|---|---|
| 研 | 研 | 研 | 研 | 研 | 研 | yán |
| 究 | 究 | 究 | 究 | 究 | 究 | jiū |
| 早 | 早 | 早 | 早 | 早 | 早 | zǎo |
| 谈 | 谈 | 谈 | 谈 | 谈 | 谈 | tán |
| 翻 | 翻 | 翻 | 翻 | 翻 | 翻 | fān |

172

| | | | | | | |
|---|---|---|---|---|---|---|
| 译 | 译 | 译 | 译 | 译 | 译 | yì |
| 能 | 能 | 能 | 能 | 能 | 能 | néng |
| 深 | 深 | 深 | 深 | 深 | 深 | shēn |
| 解 | 解 | 解 | 解 | 解 | 解 | jiě |
| 或 | 或 | 或 | 或 | 或 | 或 | huò |
| 者 | 者 | 者 | 者 | 者 | 者 | zhě |
| 就 | 就 | 就 | 就 | 就 | 就 | jiù |
| 应 | 应 | 应 | 应 | 应 | 应 | yīng |
| 该 | 该 | 该 | 该 | 该 | 该 | gāi |
| 俩 | 俩 | 俩 | 俩 | 俩 | 俩 | liǎ |
| 可 | 可 | 可 | 可 | 可 | 可 | kě |
| 容 | 容 | 容 | 容 | 容 | 容 | róng |
| 易 | 易 | 易 | 易 | 易 | 易 | yì |

| 成 | 成 | 成 | 成 | 成 | 成 | chéng |
|---|---|---|---|---|---|---|
| 竟 | 竟 | 竟 | 竟 | 竟 | 竟 | jìng |

2. 按正确的笔顺临写下列汉字:

Copy the following characters in the correct stroke-order:

| 研 | | | | | | | | | |
|---|---|---|---|---|---|---|---|---|---|
| 究 | | | | | | | | | |
| 早 | | | | | | | | | |
| 谈 | | | | | | | | | |
| 翻 | | | | | | | | | |
| 译 | | | | | | | | | |
| 能 | | | | | | | | | |
| 深 | | | | | | | | | |
| 解 | | | | | | | | | |

| 或 | | | | | | | | |
|---|---|---|---|---|---|---|---|---|
| 者 | | | | | | | | |
| 就 | | | | | | | | |
| 应 | | | | | | | | |
| 该 | | | | | | | | |
| 俩 | | | | | | | | |
| 可 | | | | | | | | |
| 容 | | | | | | | | |
| 易 | | | | | | | | |
| 成 | | | | | | | | |
| 竟 | | | | | | | | |

3. 根据拼音写出汉字:

Write out the characters that the phonetic transcriptions in the following words or phrases represent, containing each of the components given on the left:

穴： 研 jiū _____     有 kōng _____ 儿

　　　 chuān _____ 裙子

讠： tāntan _____     翻 yì _____

　　　 shuō _____     汉 yǔ _____

宀： 回 jiā _____     汉 zì _____

　　　 róng _____ 易

人： huì _____ 写汉字     jīn _____ 年

　　　 jiè _____ 绍     两 gè _____ 工人

4. 将下列各组同音字组成词语写在（　　）中：
Make up words or phrases with each of the homonymous characters in each pair and put what you have
made in the brackets:

zuò { 坐（　　　）     chéng { 城（　　　）
　　　 作（　　　）     　　　　 成（　　　）

jiā { 加（　　　）     jiù { 就（　　　）
　　 家（　　　）     　　 旧（　　　）

176

yīng { 应（　　　）　　 英（　　　）

lǐ { 里（　　　）　　 理（　　　）

yì { 译（　　　）　　 易（　　　）

jiě { 解（　　　）　　 姐（　　　）

5．写出下列词的反义词：
Give the antonym for each of the following words:

快＿＿＿＿　　早＿＿＿＿　　大＿＿＿＿

多＿＿＿＿　　对＿＿＿＿　　新＿＿＿＿

开车＿＿＿＿　　　　后边＿＿＿＿

容易＿＿＿＿　　　　问＿＿＿＿

6．给下列汉字注音，把相同的部分写在（　　）中：
Write each of the following characters in phonetic transcription and put in the brackets the component the characters in each group have in common:

哥＿＿＿＿歌＿＿＿＿　　（　　　）

成＿＿＿＿城＿＿＿＿　　（　　　）

里＿＿＿＿理＿＿＿＿　　（　　　）

票＿＿＿＿漂＿＿＿＿　　（　　　）

# 第二十七课　Lesson 27

一、汉字分析

Analysis of Characters

1. 形声字

pictophonetic characters

上形下声：

The signific component at the top, the phonetic component at the bottom, as in

筷　菜　花　究　房

2. 汉字偏旁

Character component:

待 ｛ 彳 （双人旁 shuāngrénpáng the component "彳"）
　　 寺

彳　古字表示小步慢走。

The component "彳" originated from the ideogram on the left symbolizing a person walking at an unhurried pace.

二、汉字练习

Character Exercises

178

**1.** 按正确笔顺描写下列汉字：

Trace the following characters in the correct stroke-order:

| | | | | | | |
|---|---|---|---|---|---|---|
| 始 | 始 | 始 | 始 | 始 | 始 | shǐ |
| 使 | 使 | 使 | 使 | 使 | 使 | shǐ |
| 招 | 招 | 招 | 招 | 招 | 招 | zhāo |
| 待 | 待 | 待 | 待 | 待 | 待 | dài |
| 尝 | 尝 | 尝 | 尝 | 尝 | 尝 | cháng |
| 茅 | 茅 | 茅 | 茅 | 茅 | 茅 | máo |
| 台 | 台 | 台 | 台 | 台 | 台 | tái |
| 为 | 为 | 为 | 为 | 为 | 为 | wèi |
| 健 | 健 | 健 | 健 | 健 | 健 | jiàn |
| 康 | 康 | 康 | 康 | 康 | 康 | kāng |
| 干 | 干 | 干 | 干 | 干 | 干 | gān |

| | | | | | | |
|---|---|---|---|---|---|---|
| 谊 | 谊 | 谊 | 谊 | 谊 | 谊 | yì |
| 葡 | 葡 | 葡 | 葡 | 葡 | 葡 | pú |
| 萄 | 萄 | 萄 | 萄 | 萄 | 萄 | táo |
| 试 | 试 | 试 | 试 | 试 | 试 | shì |
| 菜 | 菜 | 菜 | 菜 | 菜 | 菜 | cài |
| 筷 | 筷 | 筷 | 筷 | 筷 | 筷 | kuài |
| 化 | 化 | 化 | 化 | 化 | 化 | huà |
| 赞 | 赞 | 赞 | 赞 | 赞 | 赞 | zàn |
| 又 | 又 | 又 | 又 | 又 | 又 | yòu |
| 到 | 到 | 到 | 到 | 到 | 到 | dào |
| 楼 | 楼 | 楼 | 楼 | 楼 | 楼 | lóu |

2. 按正确笔顺临写下列汉字：
Copy the following characters in the correct stroke-order:

180

始
使
招
待
尝
茅
台
为
健
康
干
谊

| 葡 | | | | | | | |
|---|---|---|---|---|---|---|---|
| 萄 | | | | | | | |
| 试 | | | | | | | |
| 菜 | | | | | | | |
| 筷 | | | | | | | |
| 化 | | | | | | | |
| 赞 | | | | | | | |
| 又 | | | | | | | |
| 到 | | | | | | | |
| 楼 | | | | | | | |

3. 根据拼音写出汉字:

Write out the characters that the phonetic transcriptions in the following words or phrases represent, containing each of the components given at the head:

亻: 招 dài ＿＿＿＿ 会　　　　银 háng ＿＿＿＿＿

写 de＿＿＿hěn＿＿＿好

亻：jiàn＿＿＿康　　大 shǐ＿＿＿馆

文 huà＿＿＿

⺮：kuài＿＿＿子　　买 bǐ＿＿＿

回 dá＿＿＿　　　děng＿＿＿他

艹：吃 cài＿＿＿　　一束 huā＿＿＿

喝 chá＿＿＿　　Yīng＿＿＿国

pútáo＿＿＿酒

**4. 将下列各组同音字组成词语并写在（　　）中：**

Make up words or phrases with each of the homonymous characters in each pair and put what you have made in the brackets:

shǐ ｛ 使（　　　　）
　　　 始（　　　　）

shì ｛ 试（　　　　）
　　　 事（　　　　）

cháng ｛ 尝（　　　　）
　　　　 常（　　　　）

dài ｛ 待（　　　　）
　　　 代（　　　　）

kuài ｛ 快（　　　　）
　　　　 筷（　　　　）

jiǔ ｛ 九（　　　　）
　　　 酒（　　　　）

**5.** 给下列各组汉字注音，把相同的部分写在（　　）中：
Write each of the following characters in phonetic
transcription and put in the brackets the component
that the characters in each group have in common:

快＿＿＿＿筷＿＿＿＿　（　　　）

九＿＿＿＿究＿＿＿＿　（　　　）

化＿＿＿＿花＿＿＿＿　（　　　）

工＿＿＿＿空＿＿＿＿　（　　　）

子＿＿＿＿字＿＿＿＿　（　　　）

6. 试一试，在下图的空格中，各加一个汉字，每图就可组
成三个词。
Try to fill in each of the three empty boxes a character that forms with the character in the box at the
centre a word taught before:

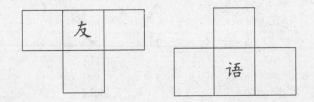

184

# 第二十八课 Lesson 28

## 一、汉字分析
### Analysis of Characters

1. 形声字

   Pictophonetic characters

   内形外声：

   The signific component enclosed in the phonetic component, as in

   问　　　闻

2. 汉字偏旁

   Character components

   冰 { 冫  （两点水 liǎngdiǎnshuǐ the component "冫"）
   　 { 水

   冫　古字象水结冰的形状。

   　　The component "冫" came from the ideogram on the left symbolizing water iced over.

   帽 { 巾  （巾字旁 jīnzìpáng the component "巾"）
   　 { 冒

  巾 古字象一块手巾。

The component "巾" originated from the ideogram on the left symbolizing a towel.

巾字旁或巾字底的字大都与纺织物品有关。

That is why the meaning of characters containing "巾" generally has something to do with textiles or fabrics.

二、汉字练习

Character Exercises

1. 按正确的笔顺描写下列汉字:

Trace the following characters in the correct stroke-order:

| | | | | | | |
|---|---|---|---|---|---|---|
| 足 | 足 | 足 | 足 | 足 | 足 | zú |
| 球 | 球 | 球 | 球 | 球 | 球 | qiú |
| 赛 | 赛 | 赛 | 赛 | 赛 | 赛 | sài |
| 昨 | 昨 | 昨 | 昨 | 昨 | 昨 | zuó |

| | | | | | | |
|---|---|---|---|---|---|---|
| 办 | 办 | 办 | 办 | 办 | 办 | bàn |
| 签 | 签 | 签 | 签 | 签 | 签 | qiān |
| 证 | 证 | 证 | 证 | 证 | 证 | zhèng |
| 队 | 队 | 队 | 队 | 队 | 队 | duì |
| 赢 | 赢 | 赢 | 赢 | 赢 | 赢 | yíng |
| 输 | 输 | 输 | 输 | 输 | 输 | shū |
| 比 | 比 | 比 | 比 | 比 | 比 | bǐ |
| 裁 | 裁 | 裁 | 裁 | 裁 | 裁 | cái |
| 判 | 判 | 判 | 判 | 判 | 判 | pàn |
| 公 | 公 | 公 | 公 | 公 | 公 | gōng |
| 平 | 平 | 平 | 平 | 平 | 平 | píng |
| 气 | 气 | 气 | 气 | 气 | 气 | qì |
| 踢 | 踢 | 踢 | 踢 | 踢 | 踢 | tī |

| | | | | | | |
|---|---|---|---|---|---|---|
| 李 | 李 | 李 | 李 | 李 | 李 | lǐ |
| 顶 | 顶 | 顶 | 顶 | 顶 | 顶 | dǐng |
| 帽 | 帽 | 帽 | 帽 | 帽 | 帽 | mào |
| 双 | 双 | 双 | 双 | 双 | 双 | shuāng |
| 冰 | 冰 | 冰 | 冰 | 冰 | 冰 | bīng |
| 鞋 | 鞋 | 鞋 | 鞋 | 鞋 | 鞋 | xié |
| 冬 | 冬 | 冬 | 冬 | 冬 | 冬 | dōng |
| 滑 | 滑 | 滑 | 滑 | 滑 | 滑 | huá |

2. 按正确的笔顺临写下列汉字:
Copy the following characters in the correct stroke-order:

| | | | | | | |
|---|---|---|---|---|---|---|
| 足 | | | | | | |
| 球 | | | | | | |
| 赛 | | | | | | |

| 昨 | | | | | | | |
|---|---|---|---|---|---|---|---|
| 办 | | | | | | | |
| 签 | | | | | | | |
| 证 | | | | | | | |
| 队 | | | | | | | |
| 赢 | | | | | | | |
| 输 | | | | | | | |
| 比 | | | | | | | |
| 裁 | | | | | | | |
| 判 | | | | | | | |
| 公 | | | | | | | |
| 平 | | | | | | | |

| 气 | | | | | | | |
| 踢 | | | | | | | |
| 李 | | | | | | | |
| 顶 | | | | | | | |
| 帽 | | | | | | | |
| 双 | | | | | | | |
| 冰 | | | | | | | |
| 鞋 | | | | | | | |
| 冬 | | | | | | | |
| 滑 | | | | | | | |

3. 给下列各组汉字注音，把相同的偏旁写在（　　）中：
Write each of the following characters in phonetic transcription and put in the brackets the component that the characters in each group have in common:

昨____晚____明____时____（　　　）

签____ 筷____ 笔____

答____ 等____（    ）

辅____ 输____ 轻____（    ）

行____ 待____ 很____（    ）

**根据拼音写出汉字：**

Write out the characters that the phonetic transcriptions in the following words or phrases stand for:

裁pàn _____          两点三kè _____

dào _____ 大使馆      bié _____ 听他的

bīng _____ 鞋        zhǔn _____ 备

hé _____ 边          huá _____ 冰

xǐ zǎo ____ ____     yóu yǒng ____ ____

tī _____ 足球        tiào _____ 舞

gēn _____ 他一起

足球 duì _____        学 yuàn _____

4. 把下列同音字组成词语并写在（    ）中：
   Make up words or phrases with each of the homonymous characters in each pair and put what you have made in the brackets:

191

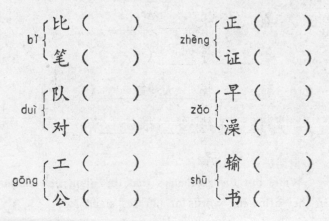

$$bǐ \begin{cases} 比（\quad） \\ 笔（\quad） \end{cases} \qquad zhēng \begin{cases} 正（\quad） \\ 证（\quad） \end{cases}$$

$$duì \begin{cases} 队（\quad） \\ 对（\quad） \end{cases} \qquad zǎo \begin{cases} 早（\quad） \\ 澡（\quad） \end{cases}$$

$$gōng \begin{cases} 工（\quad） \\ 公（\quad） \end{cases} \qquad shū \begin{cases} 输（\quad） \\ 书（\quad） \end{cases}$$

5. 给下列各组词语中带黑点的汉字注音：

Write in phonetic transcription the characters marked with "·" in each group:

$$行 \begin{cases} 行\underline{\quad}李 \\ 银行\underline{\quad} \end{cases} \qquad 教 \begin{cases} 教\underline{\quad}练 \\ 教\underline{\quad}汉语 \end{cases}$$

$$大 \begin{cases} 大\underline{\quad}使 \\ 大\underline{\quad}夫 \end{cases} \qquad 还 \begin{cases} 还\underline{\quad}有一双冰鞋 \\ 还\underline{\quad}你一双冰鞋 \end{cases}$$

6. 写出由下列汉字组成的词语：

Make up a word or phrase by adding another character to each of the following characters:

天：___天 ___天 ___天 ___天

饭：___饭 ___饭 ___饭 ___饭

开：开___ 开___ 开___

# 第二十九课　Lesson 29

一、汉字分析
Analysis of Characters

1. 形声字
   Pictophonetic characters

下形上声：
The signific component at the bottom, the phonetic component at the top, as in

愿　忘　照　努

外形内声：
The phonetic component enclosed in the signific component, as in

远　园　店

2. 汉字偏旁
   Character component

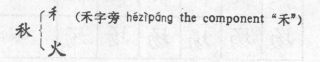

秋　⌈禾　（禾字旁 hézìpáng the component "禾"）
　　⌊火

禾 (禾) 古字象谷穗熟了下垂。

The component "禾" is a variant of the character "禾" developed from the ideogram on the left symbolizing a dropping ear of ripe grain.

禾字旁的汉字大都与粮食作物有关。如"秋"是谷物成熟的季节。

So most characters containing "禾" have something to do with grain crops. The character, "秋", for example, means "autumn", referring to the season for the year's harvest.

二、汉字练习

Character Exercises

1. 按正确笔顺描写下列汉字：

Trace the following characters in the correct stroke-order:

| | | | | | | |
|---|---|---|---|---|---|---|
| 飞 | 飞 | 飞 | 飞 | 飞 | 飞 | fēi |
| 机 | 机 | 机 | 机 | 机 | 机 | jī |
| 场 | 场 | 场 | 场 | 场 | 场 | chǎng |

194

| | | | | | | |
|---|---|---|---|---|---|---|
| 别 | 别 | 别 | 别 | 别 | 别 | bié |
| 愿 | 愿 | 愿 | 愿 | 愿 | 愿 | yuàn |
| 离 | 离 | 离 | 离 | 离 | 离 | lí |
| 忘 | 忘 | 忘 | 忘 | 忘 | 忘 | wàng |
| 所 | 所 | 所 | 所 | 所 | 所 | suǒ |
| 步 | 步 | 步 | 步 | 步 | 步 | bù |
| 努 | 努 | 努 | 努 | 努 | 努 | nǔ |
| 力 | 力 | 力 | 力 | 力 | 力 | lì |
| 站 | 站 | 站 | 站 | 站 | 站 | zhàn |
| 紧 | 紧 | 紧 | 紧 | 紧 | 紧 | jǐn |
| 注 | 注 | 注 | 注 | 注 | 注 | zhù |
| 身 | 身 | 身 | 身 | 身 | 身 | shēn |
| 体 | 体 | 体 | 体 | 体 | 体 | tǐ |

| | | | | | | |
|---|---|---|---|---|---|---|
| 放 | 放 | 放 | 放 | 放 | 放 | fàng |
| 过 | 过 | 过 | 过 | 过 | 过 | guò |
| 夏 | 夏 | 夏 | 夏 | 夏 | 夏 | xià |
| 秋 | 秋 | 秋 | 秋 | 秋 | 秋 | qiū |
| 路 | 路 | 路 | 路 | 路 | 路 | lù |
| 安 | 安 | 安 | 安 | 安 | 安 | ān |

2. 按正确的笔顺临写下列汉字：
Copy the following characters in the correct stroke-order:

| | | | | | | | |
|---|---|---|---|---|---|---|---|
| 飞 | | | | | | | |
| 机 | | | | | | | |
| 场 | | | | | | | |
| 别 | | | | | | | |
| 愿 | | | | | | | |

離

忘

所

步

努

力

站

緊

注

身

体

放

| 过 | | | | | | | |
|---|---|---|---|---|---|---|---|
| 夏 | | | | | | | |
| 秋 | | | | | | | |
| 路 | | | | | | | |
| 安 | | | | | | | |

3. 根据拼音写出带下列偏旁的汉字：

Put the phonetic transcriptions in each of the following groups of words and phrases into Chinese, containing the component given on the left:

禾 ： qiū _____天　　　我 hé___ ___他

扌 ： 机 chǎng_____　　　chéng ____ __外

　　　 dì _____址

木 ： 飞 jī_____　　　lóu _____上

　　　 yǐ _____子　　　jú _____子水

辶 ： 很 yuǎn_____　　　请 jìn_____

　　　 sòng_____她　　　欢 yíng_____

难 guò_____

心：yuàn yì_____ _____     wàng_____记

gǎn_____谢         杂 zhì_____

4. 写出由下列汉字组成的词语：
Make up a word or phrase by adding another character to each of the following characters：

上：上_____  上_____

飞：飞_____  飞_____

有：有_____  有_____  有_____

有_____  有_____

5. 把下列各组同音字组成词语并写在（    ）中：
Make up words or phrases with each of the homonymous characters in each pair and put what you have
made in the brackets：

shēn ｛ 身（    ）     bù ｛ 步（    ）
      深（    ）          不（    ）

yuàn ｛ 愿（    ）     zhù ｛ 住（    ）
      院（    ）          注（    ）

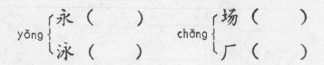

yǒng $\left\{\begin{array}{l}永 （\qquad） \\ 泳 （\qquad）\end{array}\right.$　　chǎng $\left\{\begin{array}{l}场 （\qquad） \\ 厂 （\qquad）\end{array}\right.$

6. 猜字谜：

Guess the riddle about a Chinese character:

左边一个人，右边一个本，

你想学写字，一人写一本。

（猜一汉字，谜底见下课。

The solution to the riddle is a Chinese

character given in Lesson 30.)

7. 试一试，在"学"字四边的空格中各写一个汉字，组成四个学过的词：

.Try to put in each empty box a character that forms with the character "学" given in the centre a word you have been taught：

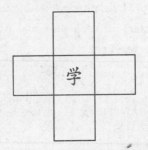

（答案见下课。

The four words to be made

are given in Lesson 30.)

200

# 第三十课 Lesson 30

一、汉字分析
Analysis of Characters

1. 形声字

Pictophonetic characters

形声字约占全部汉字的百分之九十以上。由于语言不断发展，现在很多形声字已经不能靠声旁确定它的读法。但是了解汉字的这一造字方法，对于认读汉字还是很有帮助的。形旁和声旁的结合类型归纳起来有下面六种：

Pictophonetic characters make up over 90 per cent of the total number of Chinese characters. But as the language has undergone continuous changes over the centuries the phonetic component of a great many pictophonetic characters is no longer a reliable guide to their pronunciation. Some knowledge of this aspect of the structure of Chinese characters, however, will prove useful to the learners

Following are the six main ways of combining the signific and phonetic components:

| 例 字<br>Examples | 形旁和声旁的结合类型<br>Types of combination of signific and<br>phonetic components |
|---|---|
| 泳 | 左边三点水是形旁，右边"永"是声旁<br>Signific component on the left of phonetic component. |
| 期 | 右边"月"是形旁，左边"其"是声旁。<br>Signific component on the right of phonetic component. |
| 筷 | 上边"⺮"是形旁，下边"快"是声旁。<br>Signific component on top of phonetic component. |
| 想 | 下边"心"是形旁，上边"相"是声旁。<br>Signific component below phonetic component. |
| 园 | 外边"囗"是形旁，里边"元"是声旁。<br>Phonetic component enclosed in signific component. |
| 问 | 里边"口"是形旁，外边"门"是声旁。<br>Signific component enclosed in phonetic component. |

这六类，第一类是最普遍的。

Of all six types, the first one is the most common.

## 2. 汉字偏旁

Character component

情
(feeling)
｛忄（竖心旁 shùxīnpáng the component "忄"）
青

竖心旁的字大都表示人的思想感情。

The meaning of characters containing "忄" usually refers to a person's thought, feeling or mental state.

## 3. 学过的汉字偏旁小结：

A summary of the Chinese characters so far dealt with:

| 偏　旁 Components | | 例　字 | 偏　旁 Components | | 例　字 |
|---|---|---|---|---|---|
| 形状 Shapes | 名　称 Names | Examples | 形状 Shapes | 名　称 Names | Examples |
| 亻 | 单人旁 | 你　住 | 讠 | 言字旁 | 说　话 |
| 女 | 女字旁 | 妈　娘 | 辶 | 走之旁 | 进　迎 |
| 口 | 口字旁 | 吃　喝 | 走 | 走字旁 | 起 |
| 心 | 心字底 | 想　愿 | 𧾷 | 足字旁 | 跳　踢 |
| 忄 | 竖心旁 | 情　懂 | 扌 | 提手旁 | 打　接 |

| | | | | | | | |
|---|---|---|---|---|---|---|---|
| 攵 | 反文旁 | 教 | 放 | 冫 | 两点水 | 冰 | 准 |
| 艹 | 草字头 | 菜 | 花 | 火 | 火字旁 | 炼 | 烟 |
| 竹 | 竹字头 | 笔 | 筷 | 灬 | 四点底 | 照 | 热 |
| 阝 | 右耳旁 | 那 | 都 | 土 | 土字旁 | 地 | 城 |
| 阝 | 左耳旁 | 院 | 队 | 日 | 日字旁 | 晚 | 明 |
| 饣 | 食字旁 | 馆 | 饭 | 月 | 月字旁 | 期 | |
| 衤 | 衣字旁 | 衬 | 衫 | 月 | 肉月旁 | 腿 | 朋 |
| 礻 | 示字旁 | 祝 | 视 | 王 | 王字旁 | 理 | 球 |
| 宀 | 宝盖头 | 家 | 室 | 广 | 广字头 | 店 | 康 |
| 穴 | 穴字头 | 究 | 空 | 人 | 人字头 | 今 | 会 |
| 钅 | 金字旁 | 银 | 锻 | 巾 | 巾字旁 | 帽 | 常 |
| 木 | 木字旁 | 椅 | 楼 | 纟 | 绞丝旁 | 练 | 绍 |
| 氵 | 三点水 | 河 | 洗 | 刂 | 立刀旁 | 刻 | 到 |

| 口 | 国字框 | 国 | 图 | 彳 | 双立人 | 行 | 待 |
|---|---|---|---|---|---|---|---|
| 门 | 门字框 | 间 | 问 | 力 | 力字旁 | 加 | 努 |
| 石 | 石字旁 | 矿 | 研 | 禾 | 禾字旁 | 秋 | 和 |

二、汉字练习

Character Exercises

1. 按正确的笔顺描写下列汉字：

Trace the following characters in the correct stroke-order:

| | | | | | | |
|---|---|---|---|---|---|---|
| 笑 | 笑 | 笑 | 笑 | 笑 | 笑 | xiào |
| 东 | 东 | 东 | 东 | 东 | 东 | dōng |
| 西 | 西 | 西 | 西 | 西 | 西 | xī |
| 哭 | 哭 | 哭 | 哭 | 哭 | 哭 | kū |
| 热 | 热 | 热 | 热 | 热 | 热 | rè |
| 情 | 情 | 情 | 情 | 情 | 情 | qíng |
| 自 | 自 | 自 | 自 | 自 | 自 | zì |

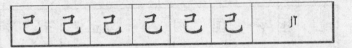

2. 按正确的笔顺临写下列汉字：
   Copy the following characters in the correct stroke-
   order:

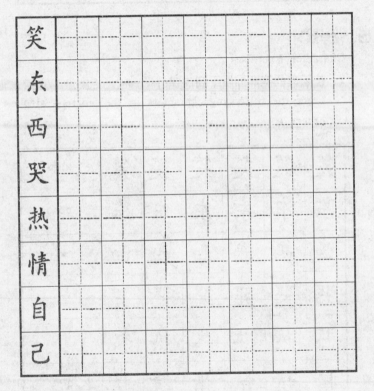

3. 根据拼音写出汉字：
   Write out the characters that each of the following
   phonetic transcriptions stand for:

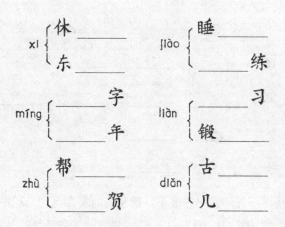

xī {休 ＿＿＿  东 ＿＿＿

jiào {睡 ＿＿＿  ＿＿＿ 练

míng {＿＿＿ 字  ＿＿＿ 年

liàn {＿＿＿ 习  锻 ＿＿＿

zhù {帮 ＿＿＿  ＿＿＿ 贺

diǎn {古 ＿＿＿  几 ＿＿＿

**4.** 写出由下列汉字组成的词语：

Write out the words or phrases made up of the character given at the head of each group and one of your own:

年： ＿＿＿＿　＿＿＿＿　＿＿＿＿

儿： ＿＿＿＿　＿＿＿＿　＿＿＿＿

　　 ＿＿＿＿　＿＿＿＿　＿＿＿＿

子： ＿＿＿＿　＿＿＿＿　＿＿＿＿

　　 ＿＿＿＿　＿＿＿＿　＿＿＿＿

边： ＿＿＿＿　＿＿＿＿　＿＿＿＿

　　 ＿＿＿＿　＿＿＿＿　＿＿＿＿

上： ＿＿＿＿　＿＿＿＿　＿＿＿＿

家：＿＿＿　＿＿＿

＿＿＿　＿＿＿

文：＿＿＿　＿＿＿　＿＿＿

＿＿＿　＿＿＿

学：＿＿＿　＿＿＿　＿＿＿

**5.** 找出下面的错字并改正，把正确的写在（　　）中：

Pick out the wrongly written characters in the following words and phrases, then write the correct forms in the brackets:

自巳（　　　）　　教练（　　　）

进步（　　　）　　研究（　　　）

招侍（　　　）　　健康（　　　）

准备（　　　）　　热情（　　　）

新间（　　　）

（上课字谜是"体"字，组词是同学、文学、学生、学习或学院。

The solution to the riddle in Lesson 29 is the character "体". The words to be made for Exercise No. 7 are "同学"，"文学"，"学生" and "学习" 'or' "学院".）

《实用汉语课本》第一册

## 汉字练习本

（英文译释）

·

北 京 语 言 学 院　编

商 务 印 书 馆 出 版

（中国北京王府井大街36号　邮政编码100710）

中国科学院印刷厂印刷

中国国际图书贸易总公司发行

（中国国际书店）

中国北京邮政信箱第399号　邮政编码100044

1982年9月第1版

1999年2月北京 第8次印刷

ISBN　7-100-00092-0／G·17

01300

9—E—1677PA